Lola Aola Seery – 1940

WHISPERING WINDS

Collected Poems of
Aola Seery Vandergriff

Poems by Lola Aola Seery Vandergriff
Copyright © 2025 The Heirs of Aola Seery Vandergriff. Edited
and compiled by her daughter, Rebecca Lynn Williams, from
Aola's published and unpublished works.

Dedicated to Aola's grandson,
Michael James-Patrick Williams

KTOK RADIO STATION
OKLAHOMA CITY, OK

Aola Seery introducing her poetry on Station KTOK
Oklahoma City, Oklahoma – 1939

You, dreamer…
To you I bring the embodiment of all your dreaming
Through the beauty of words.

You, who have not had the chance to dream…
I bring the divine spark to start the fire of inspiration.

You, little child…
I close the gates between childhood and the other world.
To you belong the words of Fairyland.

And to you, someone like me…
I would bring to you some word,
Some line of sympathy in time of sorrow…
Of laughter in time of tears.

And to all of you…

Good morning!

TABLE OF CONTENTS

REFLECTIONS AND INTROSPECTIONS .. 1

Whisperings Among the Leaves 2
Dear Dreamer 2
Indecision 3
Dream Ship 4
A Rose 4
Amulet 5
Pagan 5
Enchantment 6
Creation 7
Living 8
Moods 8
Storm 9
Bondage 9
Ladies 10
All These Am I 10
Changeling 11
Mist o' Magic 12
I Am I 13
I Would Like to Write 14
Dress Rehearsal 15
If I Could Build a Mind 15
I Wonder 16
A Ghost 16
They 17
My Gifts 18
Queer Heart 19
Sounds 20
Summer's Child 22
Will-o'-the-Wisp 23
The Comforter 24
Thoughts 24
Stay at Home 25
Roses and Thorns 26
Queen for a Day 26
I Fain Would Dance 28
Mermaid and Mortal 28

Shells 29
Chained 30
Dreams 31
The Dream 31
The Credulous 32
Advice to a Young Poet 32
Dream Clouds 33
Three in a Room 34
I Am Gypsy 36
Bewitched 38
Wings of the Wind 40
My Masterpiece 40
Through the Centuries 42

LOVE AND MARRIAGE 45

The Color of His Eyes 46
The Stranger 46
My Sun, My Moon, My Stars 47
When Day Brings 48
Cornerstone 48
Dream-Builder 49
Enough for Me 49
Dream Riches 50
On Her Wedding Day 51
The Poet 52
Second Helping 52
To Know You Are There 53
Compensation 54
Tintype 54
A Flower from A Bride's Bouquet 55
Hearth Fire 56
Homecoming 56
Silences 57
When You Are Away 58
The Letter 58
First Love 59
Words Unspoken 59
A Wishing Kiss 60

TABLE OF CONTENTS

Blue Dream 60
Together 61
Him Will I Love 62
New Lamps for Old 62
This Gift for Life's December 63
Here Are My Dreams 63
Promises 64
The Bride 64
A Shield 66
Information 67
Two Loves 68
Reserve 68
There is Such a Thing 69
Just That Way 70
When They Are Near 70
I Thee Endow 71
Prelude 72
Mirror, Mirror 73
My Life Had Need 74
A Valentine 76
Effervescence 77

FATHERS, MOTHERS AND CHILDREN .. 79

A Name 80
Grapevine Swing 81
Mud Pies 82
Lessons in Kite Flying 83
Five 84
Heartbreak at Six 84
My Goblin Child 85
Stormy 85
Mother 86
Coffee Break 87
Pockets 88
Elmiry 88
Prodigy 89
Wisdom 89
Tiptoe Time 90

Fiddle-Footed Cowpoke 90
Fairy Grandmas 91
Close to the Stars 91
Following a Star 92
Featherstitched In Blue 92
Dream-Shiner-Upper 93
Lost Mother 93
Ma! 94
How Much I Envy You 94
Milady 94
Tiger, Tiger 95
Mother-Fond 96
Love Triangle 97
Schoolyard 97
Refugees 98
To Michael 99
Why 100
In This Room 102
No Less a King 104
The Old Ways 105
Wee Know-Nothing-Curly-Head 106
Moon Madness 107
Lullaby Lady 108
Catalpa School, First Grade 109
Madonna in a Blue Gown 110
The Fiddler 111
The Drum 112
To a Teenage Son 113
Quilts 114
Little, Dirty, Ragged Urchin 115
Somebody's Spoiled the Baby 116
School Days 117
This Is the Day 118
Christmas, 1967 119
Borne on the Wind 120
Of Kingdoms 120
A Cradle Rocking 121
Who Tends a Tree 122

TABLE OF CONTENTS

Father-Mother 123
Lullaby 124
What to Name the Baby 125
Mother's China Plate 126
Farewell 127
Heritage of Hills – Class of 1939 128

TOIL AND PERSEVERANCE ***131***

Shadows 132
While Others Sleep 133
Oklahoma Father 134
Winter Respite 135
A Farm Woman's Diary 136
Ladder of Life 138
Sing Me a Love Song 139
Four Ages 139
Retirement 140
Her Hands 140
Wings for Her Feet 141
Her 'n' Me 142
Woman's World 143
Futility 144

HOME AND HOLIDAYS ***145***

The Beckoning Light 146
Declining an Invitation to Dinner 146
Star Wishes 147
A Little House 147
Remembering Wee Homes 148
You, Who Lived Here 148
Interior Decorating 149
Fences 149
An Empty Heart 150
The Shepherd 150
My House 151
Home 151
Ghost House 152
Sacrilege 153

Ever Since I Came 154
Thanksgiving 154
The Star 155
Dear Santa 156
A Crooked Christmas Tree 157
A Tree in a Trailer Window 158
One Candle 159
Faith 160
The Tiniest Evergreen 160
I Saw the Child King 162
The Empty Stocking 164
The New Year 165
New Years – 1937 166
The House That Jack Built 168
Wanted: A House 169
Through the Gap in the Hedge 170
Blue Door to Nowhere 172

NONSENSE ***173***

The Sneep 174
Death of an India Rubber Man 174
My Heart Lies in the Sun 175
Temptation 175
A Writer's Chains 176
Unclaimed Treasure 176
Turn About 176
Genius 177
The Trillipede 177
Quadropotamus 178
Fantasy 178
Intentions 179
The Unicarp 179
Trisexoderm 179
Would-be Sinner 180
They Say 180
Short Short Story 180
TV 180
If This Be Your Idea 181

TABLE OF CONTENTS

Mother's Prayer 181
To Hear You 181
Housework 182
Problem in Higher Mathematics 182
What Shadows Do 183
Waterlogged 183
Claustrophobia 183
Joe Bill Garrett 184
Pals 184
Mother - Poet 185
To an Erring Relative 185
Awkward Angel 185
The Cabbage and the Rose 186
My Sins and I 187
Comparison 188
Secrets 188
I 188
Revenge 189
Survival 189
Conformity 190

TIMES AND PLACES ***191***

Last Night 192
Wings 192
I Remember a Time 193
Heritage 193
Laughter 194
Spring 194
Anew In Springtime 194
Memories 195
You, Oklahoma 196
Royalty 197
Flying South 197
Leaves 198
Eternal Change 198
Prairie Pictures of Autumn 199
Freeway 200
New Fields 200

You, I Love 201
I Am the Very Only Fairy 202
Northland 203
La Selva Encantada 203
April 204
Mirror of Life 204
Jeweled Hill 204
March 205
In the Hollows 206
Sunset 206
Home Work 207
Moon Tears 208
When Today is Yesterday 210
One Brief Hour of April 211
Mushroom Towns 212
Progress 212
The Wanderer Returns 213
First Snow 214
Salute 214
The Entrance to Fairy Land 215
Peaceful Hollow 216
An Interview with Dame Nature 216
Prairies 217
Fairy Music 218
April Fool 218
Thank You Note 219
Two Songs 220
Old Trails 222

LOSS AND SORROW ***223***

A Dark Moon, Always 224
The Door to My Heart 224
Coffined 225
Tonight 226
I Wish I Knew 226
Ghost-Love 227
Portrait from a Castle Wall 228
Yesterday 229

TABLE OF CONTENTS

Winter 229	Transformation 255
A Chilling Rain 230	A Woman Scorned 256
Why Do I Sigh? 230	Half-A-Child 257
Why Do I Weep? 231	Sometimes 258
Seeking an Ember 232	Katie of the Salt Marsh 258
Bitter Autumn 233	Selling Memories 260
Chilly Winds 233	Someone Should Have Told You 261
Mourning 234	Waiting 262
There Is No Place 234	The Second Prayer 262
Forgotten Youth 235	You Will Not Know 263
Discontent 236	Somehow I Do Remember 264
Footsteps 237	Mist Against the Window 264
A Stranger to These Ways 238	I, Who Remember 265
Filing 239	It Will Not Seem Strange 265
A Moment There 239	The Disillusioned 266
Never Cry 240	Of Kings and Courage 266
Two-Ways-Going 240	With Only Wonder 267
Perfection 241	Do Not Dream Back 268
Spinster 241	Ghost Child's Face 269
Today 242	Shadow - Bond 270
Last Night I Dreamed 242	What Broke Then? 271
A Man Wants a Son 242	The Last Whip-Poor-Will 271
The Fisher's Wife 244	Bittersweet 272
Scottish Ballad 245	***WAR AND CONFLICT 273***
Might Have Been 245	
Divorce - An Abstract Impression ... 246	If You Should Go to Fight 274
Why Have You Come to Awaken Me? 247	Don't Let Your Heart Go South 274
Growing Blind 247	An Empire Falls 275
Now 248	Leopold 276
Quest 248	Hold Hard to All Good Things 276
I Shall Write Again 249	Lend Lease 277
Retribution 250	The Right to Bear Arms 278
Unstrung 250	I Sat Upon a Quiet Hill 279
Pray, Be Kinder 251	Again 280
The Precipice of Silence 252	A Mother's Vigil 280
I Must Remember 253	War 281
Buried Treasure 254	Thirst 282
I Shall Not Miss You 254	God's Child 284

TABLE OF CONTENTS

Two Mothers 285
Who Goes There? 286
The Name of Spain 288
Peacemaker 288
The Shadow Place 289
Independence Day 290
Dictator 291
Czechoslovakia 292
Holland, May 14th, 1940 293
Trampled Dreams 294
Duel in Simmon's Swamp 295
Valentines Day – 1918 296
Comrade Unremembered 297
The Grandeur of Spain 298
The Confederate 299
Every Day at Sundown 300
Monuments 300
Cycle 301
Rain 302
John Smith – 1880 to 1929 303

BROTHERHOOD *305*

To Whom It May Concern 306
Color Line 307
One God 308
White Mist Rising 308
Indian Maid 309
Desecration 310
Cherokee Prophecy 311
Because Someone Did Not Forget 312
To a Tom Tom 313
Little Papoose 314
The Eagle and the Dove 315
Trail of Tears 316
Cliff Dwelling 316
Singing Bird 317

NATURE *319*

Fall of the King 320
This is the Sea 320
The Black Pony 321
Snow 322
My Friend, Storm 322
Whip-Poor-Will 323
Enchanted Garden 324
How Does Your Garden Grow? 325
The Gallery 326
Limitations 327
Black Earth Love 328
A Garden 329
October's Oklahoma 330
The Quiet Hour 331

AGING *333*

One Dream 334
Understanding 335
Grow Old Gracefully 336
Still Those Tints Abide 336
Cornstalk Fiddle 337
Day's End 338
Reverie in Rain 338
Growing Weather 339
Spring Comes Out of January 340
The Little Hills 341
Sunbonnet Sue 342
This Is My Sign 343

PASSING *345*

If I Should Go 346
The Shadowed Stair 346
Insight 347
Ebbtide 348
Now in November 348

TABLE OF CONTENTS

To Question Why 348
Where I Shall Lie 349
Pastel Fairies 349
Fear 350
The Song of the Pinewood Tree 351
Not the Way of You 352
Nine Pins 352
Where Shamrocks Grow 353
Fools 354
Prisoner 355
Don't Be Afraid 356
Hospital Waiting Room 357
Death Is Like a Paneled Door 358
To Fifty Years 358
Soul-Strings 359
You Grieve - I Sing 360
Folded Wings 360
Spiritual Rest 361
Derelict 361
Singing in the Sun 362

FAITH *363*

Belief 364
Home at Twilight 364
Resurrection 365
Prayer Perfect 366
The Fisherman 366
For Jesus 367
High Noon 368
Man of Galilee 369
Country Church 370
The Gift of Flowers 372
Little Boy Lost 372
Pioneers 373
The Message 374
Crucifixion 374
The Touch of His Hand 375

Prayer 376
Glory 376
Man-Made 377
Peace 378
Not for This 378
I Found Peace 379
Judgment Day 380
My Prayer 382
Salvation 384
God's World 386
The Return 387
Foundations 388
The Great Master 389
And Who Shall Say 389
My Multi-colored Mutt 390
Peasant's Prayer 391
Hermit 391
God's Handiwork 392
These Hands 392
Philosophy 393
Guidance 394
The Things He Must Have Done 395
Golden Harvest 396
A Dream 397
The Cross Man 398
The Last Mile of the Way 400
He Prays 402
God Understands 403
You, Scientist 404
Re-Incarnation 404
The Ultimate 405
Woven Threads 406
Hoffman's Portrait of the Christ Child 407
Suburban Spring 408
Peter Was a Good Man 410
Summation 411

REFLECTIONS AND INTROSPECTIONS

Aola Vandergriff
Oklahoma Daydreaming, 1943

Whisperings Among the Leaves

The tree tops sigh, filled with old whisperings,
Whisperings which have lived
Through all eternity,
And face infinity.
From the far corners of the wood
I hear them. Hear!
A faint, sweet trill,
They begin
To be taken up by tree after tree,
The muted music of the organ of the forest.
Then silence
While the whole world quivers
With the beauty of the sound.
Whispering trees,
Teach to me the words
And the music of thy caroling,
That I may add to the beauty of thy song
In the hush of the evening,
My few faint whisperings
Among the leaves.

Dear Dreamer

So soft at my door there came knocking a dreamer
Crying so piteously, "Dear lady come,
Come and lend me a dream, Ma'am, a dream of thy making
For I have awakened, and summer is gone.

"All summer I watched the wildflowers on the hillside,
Watched them and wove them into a dream of my own,
But this morning I waked to a chill burst of autumn,
And now I must die for my dreams are all flown."

"Dear dreamer," I answered in studious fashion,
"The stray wisps of snow do but cover thy dreams,
Like the locks of the aged in crystalline splendor.
Who'd want a cherry while yet it was green?

"When you wove your dream of the flowers on the hillside,
You wove not their souls with the bright colored thread.
You saw not how weary they stood after springtime.
They must rest like we mortals. Your dreams are not dead."

*****Aola Seery, published at age 17,
Golden Harvest, Mistletoe Press, 1937*****

Indecision

I was but set to follow single stars,
But, whirling, on each side around me rise
The stars and leave me standing in surprise,
With planets, spheres, the whole sky in my eyes.

How many more in life have been so set,
And seeing stars in blue space from a hill,
Dazed, wish for all, not one, and wish until
The stars have fled and left them standing still.

Dream Ship

It's so much fun to be alone
And tell my thoughts to me
And dream of ships a-sailing
Though I'm so far from the sea.
And all my ships have silver sails
While none have canvas spread.
My ships have golden cargo
And to the moon are sped.

My ships have golden cargo.
They fly before the gale,
And there is no embargo
In the land to which they sail.
But ships must have a captain,
And captains need a crew.
Though it's such fun to be alone,
I'll sail my ship with you.

***** Aola Seery, published at age 17,
Golden Harvest, Mistletoe Press, 1937*****

A Rose

A rose,
Unfolding dewy petals to the sky,
And shaking out her silken robes that I
Might see and gladder be as I pass by.
It grows.

A thought,
A thing of beauty on the printed page
Of yellowed parchment and worn with age,
The philosophy that some old, learned sage
Had taught.

They're kin,
The roses and the thoughts.

Who better knows?
For it was I who searched the dusty rows
Of books - found both the briar and the rose
Therein.

***** Aola Seery, published at 17,
Golden Harvest, Mistletoe Press, 1937*****

Amulet

This day has been a hectic one, and yet,
When tomorrow has erased the stain away
Of bitterness and worry's strain away,
I'll add some moment to the amulet
Of memory I wear to hold each day
That it not slip away,
Unlived, away.

Pagan

The fairies chose you for their very own,
You, with your startled eyes and elfin ways,
But swift, too swift, the midnight hour was flown,
And you were left to tread life's mortal maze.

You, who were meant to laugh upon the wind
Where blossoms blow and bluebells sway and chime,
For you was meant an immortality
In the fairyland of Once-Upon-A-Time.

But oft a midnight sudden turns, and then
You cannot hide a start of swift surprise,
And the lost souls of eternity cry out
In the strangeness of your startled pagan eyes.

Enchantment

The wind blew all the real away
And left enchantment straying,
Elfin eyes and sandaled feet,
And strange, sweet music playing.
Some Pixie being touched my eyes,
Gave me its small, cool hand.
"Come mortal, you will be the first
To gaze on fairyland."

The wind blew back reality,
Sent dreams and visions flying.
I found a small dream yesterday,
Some careless breeze left lying.
It brought back dreams of fairyland …
Would they had let me stay.
I can't forget my happiness
'Fore dreamland blew away.

I'll ever walk in memory
Through weird trees strange and tall,
Feel kinship with the fairies when
I hear a hoot owl call.
Some pixie being touched my eyes
But didn't wipe them clean.
Winds blue enchantment quite away
But left me one small dream.

*****Aola Seery, published at age 17,
Golden Harvest, Mistletoe Press, 1937*****

Creation

In the beginning of creation
'Fore fish and fowl and tree,
Two half-made, formless things were asked
What they would like to be.
They gazed out o'er the half-formed world
And each gave his decree.

"I'd like to be a shadowed pool
Where only dreamers wend,
Where the rainbows of the world begin,
And all the rainbows end …
Sell my dreams to gentle dreamers
Who come with time to spend."

"I'd like," cried out the other,
"To be a shallow rill
And sing through fertile valleys,
Laugh down a grassy hill,
A clear cool leaping streamlet
Where one may drink his fill."

And so, they are forever.
The rill runs quick and cool,
Sets elfin echoes laughing,
A beloved merry fool.
But dreamers find a solace
In the shadow-haunted pool.

***** Aola Seery, published at age 17,
Golden Harvest, Mistletoe Press, 1937*****

Living

Take a measure of sun dust,
Sprinkle it over a flower.
Watch it a minute, as one must,
Or maybe a golden hour.
Strain a sieve full of star shine.
Siphon a drop of dew.
Make a daisy chain for a lifeline
To tie all your dreaming to.
Gather the petals of roses.
Prick your palm with a thorn.
And you'll link your life with the living
And all who were ever born.

Moods

The sun was high and bright, and all was blue,
No cloud, no spot, no shade to mar the sky.
And foliage flourished green where roses grew,
But sad was I.

The fog crept from the sea and shrouded trees.
The leaden sky wept slowly all the day.
The fog fey's faded roses chilled the breeze,
And I was gay.

*****Aola Seery, published at age 17,
Golden Harvest, Mistletoe Press, 1937*****

Storm

I would write with all the vibrant power
Of slashing storms, of sturdy bearded Thor,
Or weld my words together with Hell's fire,
With anvil clang, a wild Wagnerian score.
Thor's hammer I would wield, but still, instead,
In pale blue ink I pen a pale blue sonnet,
Quite woman-like, for my sex rules my head,
With pale blue words like lacy ribbons on it.
To read my work,
You'd never know I mourn
A storm
Unborn.

Bondage

Once upon a time, unwittingly I wandered
In a land of fallen suns and blinded stars
Where Faith was flown, and all the dreams were plundered…
Robbed of their glow and held by hatred's bars.

I found a small star sighing, weeping sadly,
A star that once was brightest up above.
It begged for alms and so I gave it gladly,
My one last bit of pride and faith and love.

Then suddenly, the world was bathed in glory.
I found myself from Hatred's bondage rent,
And so, I left the place … so ends my story …
And left behind me disillusionment.

****Aola Seery, published at age 17,
Golden Harvest, Mistletoe Press, 1937****

Ladies

Laced in stays of inhibition,
Long black bloomers of tradition,
Petticoats that sweep the ground,
Of moral fiber stern and sound.
My poems are ladies to the core.
My poems are ladies,
Nothing more.

Sometimes I would like to shock
Their rigid postures chock-a-block,
To deck their cheeks with wanton paint,
To spawn a Satyr, or a Saint,
But prissy prim they sit in rows
With pursy lips and tilted nose.
I add another to their score.
My poems are ladies,
Nothing more.

They should have my respect as such,
But I don't like them very much!

All These Am I

I feel a strange exultance in the cry
Of an eagle swooping swiftly to its prey,
Yet weep to see a sparrow struggle, die,
Or the red fox turn and face his foe at bay.

It is the law of life, but singing wings
And four soft feet will haunt my ceaseless springs.
My heart goes singing, singing with the lark.
My soul sighs at the soft curve of a hill,
And merges in a gray world, not yet dark,
And hears the shadows move when nights are still.
The talking leaves and grasses speak for me,
And in companionship with them is ecstasy.

I am as wild as these small forest things.
Watch, lest I change before your very eyes
And strain with all the power of beating wings
Against my body's cage, to reach the skies,
Or walk on four soft feet that long for space,
With slanting eyes in fierce, triangled face.
All these am I, but nothing, naught of man.
Man lacks the vital spark, the seeing eye.
Man has built cages since the world began,
And caged by shafts of steel and glass am I,
And I beat on these strong bars from within.
I am a sinner, then, if this be sin.

Changeling

In the twilight when the moonlight
Makes shadows halfway weird,
And the old man weaves strange legends
Of ghosts and shadows feared,

On evenings when the warm moon
Rides strangely in the sky,
We laugh and go a-dancing,
The shadows all and I.

In the twilight in the moonlight
The laughing shadows pass,
All dancing in the meadow
In the silver gilded grass.

One brings me new daffodils …
I must be going soon.
'Tis half past fairy dancing time.
Dim grows the weary moon.

When the moon goes, go the shadows,
And I am left alone.
The shadows hie them homeward,
But I, I have no home.

In the twilight in the moonlight
Have I my hour of mirth.
I am but half a shadow
And only half of earth.

***** Aola Seery, published at age 17,
Golden Harvest, Mistletoe Press, 1937*****

Mist o' Magic

The old ones have a legend that they love to sit and tell
About a mist o' magic in a haunted fairy dell.
"It takes ahold the heart of one. A witchery it weaves,"
So said the south wind sighing and whispering in the leaves.

I sought and found the fairy ring, halfway 'twixt light and gloom.
Enchanted was by sight and smell of wild crabapple bloom.
Like hordes of dainty fairies were the gay winged butterflies,
And I seemed to feel the presence of a thousand slanting eyes.

The old ones laugh at legends and try to make me see
There's no such thing as fairies, such thing as witchery.
But when the time's 'twixt light and gloom and grass with dew is wet,
The wind and I fly to the dell … believe in fairies yet.

*****Aola Seery, published at age 17,
Golden Harvest, Mistletoe Press, 1937*****

I Am I

I am I, and that is all
        I am or was ... shall ever be.
A white nun in her robes of grace,
        In pure and chaste severity.
Is this the one you see?

Or perhaps you see the fire
        That burns and flames to sink and die
And flare again in wild desire
        To burn my spirit on the sky.

Coming from my white towers down
        To meet the blaze my cold soul warms.
I see you as a little boy,
        Asleep with head on folded arms.

Though in the cobwebbed nunnery
        The ancient armors creak and rust,
And though the fires cease running free,
        From tower and woodsmoke come I must.

Oh, that I could give you peace ...
        I reach my arms to you ... a cry
Is urgent as a white tower falls
        Against the flames that reach and die.
That is all. I am I.

I Would Like to Write

I would like to write a star that wounds
And sends suns bleeding down the western sky
To speed sky lanes with scintillating sounds
'Til cruising comets falter, crash and die.

And I would write a spider, velvet clad,
To weave a web to bind my heart and hand,
To shrink myself to one soul, small and sad,
Against the dark death thoughts that dim the land.

I would write a noble steed to ride,
A wing'ed horse with nostrils all aflame,
With hooves that chip the cloudbank in his stride,
And Pegasus, yes, Pegasus his name.

Instead, I stand myopic in the night,
And all my stars have blurred and feathered edges.
My webs are silk, and gossamer, and light,
Lace to camouflage the dusty ledges.

The Pegasus that I can never write
Is Rosinante, grazing in the hedges.

Dress Rehearsal

Tiny shiny soldiers, to shrill fifes marching time,
Stand with glinting muskets in a shining line.
Attention! Dress inspection! Then all the soldiers scoff
At the ones who dress in clothes unpressed
Or left some buttons off.

My thoughts are little soldiers, which march in single file.
Some try to make a body laugh, and some to cause a smile.
Their little caps are pretty words, which soldierly they doff,
But when they march in print, I find
I've left some buttons off.

If I Could Build a Mind

If I could build a mind, I'd make a door
To close at will, against intruding things,
Against the shrieking winds, the seas that roar,
So I could hear the whisper sound of wings.

A window I would have with rainbow veils
To filter out all ugliness, all cold,
And shed sun-colors, warm against my cheek,
To keep me young forever, never old.

If I could build a mind, I'd make a door
To keep that mind refreshed, rejoiced, renewed.
The door to my mind ever stands ajar,
And things intrude … intrude … oh, things intrude!

I Wonder

Always I've wondered what I'd do
If one night strange and still,
On a bleak and lonely crossroad,
Atop some windswept hill
Where, like an ancient gallows
In sharp-etched silhouette,
A guidepost pointed out two paths …
What would I do, and yet …
I have stumbled through the rain
As branches lashed my face,
And I have learned that pain-barbed thorns
Hide in each grassy place.

A Ghost

I bathed in moonlight from the moon,
A silver coin hung in the sky,
And dressed in shadows from the gloom,
With laughter stolen from the loon.
A merry ghost was I.

To make my hands more ghostly chill
Such as befits a ghost like me,
I dip them in the sparkling rill
From snowdrifts melting on the hill.
The world's afraid of me.

I shine the lady's slippers gay
And make the blue bells ring
Whene'er I must patrol the day
For evenings they are tucked away.
It's fun to haunt in spring.

***** Aola Seery, published at age 17,
Golden Harvest, Mistletoe Press, 1937*****

They

They needn't say
That my cupboard is bare
Because it holds the nest
Of a shy wood hare.

They needn't think
That I talk to myself
'Cause they heard a daffodil
Laughing on the shelf.

How could I help it
That some came too soon
And caught me dancing
With the little, new moon?

Why should it matter
That behind my door
I keep a rainbow
Tied to the floor?

They are the queer ones
With their jealous eyes.
I, who talk with wood and sky,
Am very, very wise.

My Gifts

I come to you, and I am bearing gifts.
Oh, do not turn my gifts away unseen
Although an abyss stretches deep between.
My gifts will be there when a new dream lifts
To make a bridge across the unbridged rifts.
My gifts will be there, waiting and serene,
For when these baubles drop their blinding screen,
Then you will pause and look upon my gifts.

My first is of a time that long is past …
Of childhood days, of toiling unashamed.
My second, understanding found at last.
It has a word called patience for a frame.
My third is for tomorrow and is vast,
A single word, just love, is that gift's name.

***** Aola Seery, published at age 17,
Golden Harvest, Mistletoe Press, 1937*****

Queer Heart

To you, I am a new-carved, unstruck lyre.
You cannot understand me, never will.
You love my simple peace, but I am fire.
'Tis only to your eyes that I am chill.
'Tis strange you cannot see that I am wild
To follow, dancing, after Pagan Pan,
For I am not of earth, a fairy child,
I hide deep in two eyes and laugh at man.

Then I shall go on my way, a fairy child,
Weeping o'er my crushed and bruis'ed stars.
I go, unseen, before you on your way,
Strewing stars for you to step upon.
You cannot understand, but I shall stay
And cherish all your footprints when you've gone.
When hills have come between us and dread time
Draws his curtain, and our vision bars.

———————

Sounds

I am the keeper of little sounds
That come from the country and from the towns,
The sounds of the thunderbolts that shake
The land and the sea and the sky awake.
The sound of thunder is big and round.
Sound...
Sound...
Sound...

I am the keeper of sounds of sighs
That curve into rainbows in tear-mist skies.
They are tangled ribbons that twine and bend
For a sound of sighing has no end,
But curving from every roof they're found.
Sound ...
Sound ...
Sound ...

I am the keeper of sounds of things,
Of the zigzag sound of an eagle's wings,
Of the rippling sound of a singing stream,
The knife-keen edge of a sudden scream,
And oh, what a multitude abound …
        Sound …
                Sound …
                      Sound …

I am the keeper of things you say,
All tagged and titled and tucked away,
Of the pointed things and the organ notes.
The melodies from a million throats
Are all on a silver spindle wound.
        Sound …
                Sound …
                      Sound …

Summer's Child

Tears have I? None, oh none.
I am a child of the summer sun,
Wild and slim and dusky-eyed,
In pools of sun in hollows hide,
Run the ridges with laughing ease,
Silent, 'neath tall, shadowed trees,
Barefoot over new plowed land,
Still on a warm, high hill I stand.
Then the winds stand still, so swift I run.
I am a child of the summer sun.

I am a child of the summer moon,
In clinging shadows and silver shoon
With all the mystery of the South…
Deep in eyes, warm on mouth…
Going where the warm moon goes,
Bending here to touch a rose,
Walking paths of earth turned over,
Stepping deep in fragrant clover,
Hearing the hush'ed wind's sad croon…
I am a child of the summer moon.

And, as the summer days grow nigh,
Though the sun is faint in the still gray sky,
I know the earth will soon be pied
With hordes of daisies, golden-eyed,
And they will sway in fragrance sweet,
A springing carpet for my feet,
And I shall run where breezes run!
I am a child of the summer sun,
Near clinging shadows and silver shoon …
I am a child of the summer moon.

Will-o'-the-Wisp

A will-o'-the-wisp flies 'fore the wind
That I'm forever seeking.
There's a castle in the clouds somewhere,
But it's obscured from view.
In that place, happiness is hid.
In that place, sorrow's sleeping.

In that place of tasks rewarded,
And the place of dreams come true,
It lies beyond the pool of grief,
Beyond the give up mountain,
And it's a sore temptation
To rest beside a fountain
And leave the climb to others
Until dawns another day.

But the will-o'-the-wisp flies 'fore the wind,
And I must be swift after.
There's a promise sweet of rest complete.
I know I must not fail,
For there, across the mountain,
I can hear their merry laughter.
The will-o'-the-wisp flies 'fore the wind
And I must on its trail.

*****Aola Seery, published at age 17,
Golden Harvest, Mistletoe Press, 1937*****

The Comforter

When you have known the blight of bitter years
    Without a single golden slant of sun
And there have been no dreams, no battles won,
    Then come to me, to me with all your tears.
If you have longed for tall shields and for spears
    And for the gentle days that long are done,
To trace the course a white-winged ship has run,
    Then come, before your dreaming disappears.

My hands are gentle hands and hands of fire.
    They hold to things that are not, cannot be.
    They hold the echo of each lost desire.
Oh, bring your longings and your tears to me.
    I am all things to which you do aspire.
    I am the Comforter, true poetry.

Thoughts

I had a thought the other night,
    A very hateful thought.
My thought flew out the window,
    And the evening breezes caught

The thing and took it through the night
    Unto mine enemy,
And for that one small thought she thought
    A thousand worse of me.

Now, you see, she thought I meant that thought,
But I don't think I did.
When it flew out the window,
I wished that it were hid.

That thought in a chain of little thoughts,
Was hatred's final link.
Next time I go to think a thought,
I think I just won't think.

Stay at Home

You must come to me, Oh World, and lay thy gifts,
If gifts thou hast for me, within my door.
I love my fellow man but from afar
And find his gifts and faults in written lore.
These four walls mold my world, and should I stray
From what means peace to me and sweet content,
Ideals I'd lose and faith in human clay
And spend my life in fear, bewilderment.

These four walls hold my world. My world is small.
The world outside my world is so immense,
And lest I lose my faith in humankind,
I'll worship it across a high hedge fence.

*****Aola Seery, published at age 17,
Golden Harvest, Mistletoe Press, 1937*****

Roses and Thorns

I have a private graveyard
Where my dreams are laid to rest,
The silly and the vain ones,
The ones that I thought best.

In the tomb right next to riches,
I've buried deep success.
I've found a better substitute
By some called happiness.

I've buried dreams of beauty.
I wanted more than wealth.
I've found it now in others,
In others than myself.

I've buried wealth and with it greed
And vanity with its poses.
I planted thorn trees on their graves
And harvested red roses.

*****Aola Seery, published at age 17,
Golden Harvest, Mistletoe Press, 1937*****

Queen for a Day

I found a megic mirror once.
'Twas in the land o' Kerry.
I searched for it!
And gazed in it!
And lo! I was a fairy.
Ah, Colin, and would ye believe it!
I thought it was daft I must be.
But the shamrock grew green 'round the mirror,
So, I know that I surely was me.

Oh, I was smug and satisfied
And proud to see me wings,
And so, I played I ruled the land,
The land of stuff and things.
Ah, Colin, and don't ye believe it?
Go laugh then! The pleasure is thine.
There surely was no fairy ever
With locks half so auburn as mine.

The fairies dearly love to tease,
And a few with wings outspread
Stood just behind
As I searched to find
A gold crown for me head.
Ah, Colin, and would ye believe it?
Ah sure, I was daft not to see
That a pool was me megical mirror,
And the fairies were laughin' at me.

Next time I shall be much, much wiser,
And naught shall escape me detection.
I'll tell the true glass from the false one,
And I'll sure not be fooled by reflection.
Ah, Colin, and now ye are laughin'!
Now wouldn't ye make a fine fey
With your red hair and freckles and scoffin'!
At least I was queen for a day!

*****Aola Seery, published at age 17,
Golden Harvest, Mistletoe Press, 1937*****

I Fain Would Dance

I fain would dance along the hills, as vibrant as a flame.
Despair is heavy-footed, and despair is old and lame.
I fain would dance from spring to spring where fragrant blossoms grow.
Despair is stumble-footed, and he dreams of long ago.
Despair is lagging-footed, and he treads a measure slow.

I fain would cleave the wings of mist and dart along the hills.
Despair is clumsy-booted, and he cannot leap the rills.
I fain would fly away on wings of mist and sunset's glow.
Despair is earthy-rooted, and despair is halt and slow.
Despair holds fast my dancing heels and will not let me go.

Mermaid and Mortal

Pretty little mermaid, on a coral throne,
Brushing from thy locks the salt sea foam.
Pray lend me thy glass, pray lend me thy comb
When the tide goes out, I'll send them home.

Pretty little mortal, who-so-e'er ye be,
My glass is only a little drop in the center of the sea.
I can't give it away, for 'twould melt under mortal thumb.
As for a comb, go pluck a burr from a sea sweet gum.

*****Aola Seery, published at age 17,
Golden Harvest, Mistletoe Press, 1937*****

Shells

Next to being a fairy, I
Should like to be a shell and lie
On the golden sands beside the sea,
Moaning tropical tales of mystery,

Of mermaids diving for pearls below,
And blue lagoons, where the warm winds blow.
Weird are the tales the oceans tell
To the listening ear of a whispering shell.

*****Aola Seery, published at age 17,
Golden Harvest, Mistletoe Press, 1937*****

Chained

There's a dancing of the fairies
When the moon grows bright,
In a shade hidden glade tucked out of sight,
And the trees are gold in their moonlight dress,
And the scented breeze is a soft caress.
There's a fairy dance in the moonlight's glow,
In a hidden glade that I used to know.
But then I was fey, and then I was free.
Now the mortal world has its hold on me.

The goblins gather when the dark moon reigns,
When the sunset dies, and the starlight wanes,
And the toadstools gleam in the weird blue light
Like pale dead hands in an eerie night.
The tortured trees raise their twisted arms
Where witches work their wicked charms.

Elves down hills the great stones roll,
And I am chained by a mortal soul.
I danced in the glade in the strange bright moon,
Clad in shadows and silver shoon.
I talked with goblins in the dark moonlight
And blotted out the moon in a witch's flight.
I built a wee hut a toadstool under...
Sent stones down a hill in a roll of thunder.
But I can't go back when the two moons rise,
For I've seen the world through a mortal's eyes.

———————

Dreams

I found a tiny fragment of a dream
Left from my childhood days ... a dream so old
Its star shine had worn off and left it cold.
"Keep it," said a voice, "and watch it gleam."

I kept the dream, although it wasn't bright
And found illusions lost so long ago,
Mended broken promises to make it glow,
And was rewarded with faith's shining light.

The Dream

I am the loves of all mankind.
I am the lonely hater.
I forged a boy a bright new sword
And slew him with it later.

I built a tall cathedral, too,
To light the soul's dark winters.
I made a bomb and flung it down
And blew it into splinters.

I've lived more than ten thousand years,
Yet no more than an hour.
I am as old as man's first tears,
Young as the newest flower.

I am the fool; I am all-wise;
I am truth; I am lying.
I am the dream of all mankind,
And I have wings for flying!

The Credulous

The townsfolk told me
That those who do good
Are sure to find treasure
Hid in the wood.

I did as they bade me.
Three times a day
I knelt in my closet
And tried to pray.

I never ate meat.
I gave to the poor,
And sheltered the outcast
Who wept at my door.

I searched in the wood
'Til the shadows thinned,
With naught to break silence
But bells of the wind.

I scratched in the thorns,
I dug under loam,
But for all that I found
I might have been home.

My empty hands bled,
But the townsfolk laughed
And said I had always
Been a bit daft.

Advice to a Young Poet

Young poet, fierce and bitter in your youth,
Do not be but a waster of your day
In seeking reformations, untrue truth.
These things shall only come and pass away.

Here where the sea stands now, there once was land,
And where the land lies now, once was but sea,
And change will change although your plans be planned,
This is to be, and then it will not be.

A small bird pauses overhead to sing.
Listen and observe him, oh my brother.
He pivots on a shining feathered wing.
This dream will last as long as any other.

***** Aola Seery, published at age 17,
Golden Harvest, Mistletoe Press, 1937*****

Dream Clouds

This is my cloud, the one that drifts and seems
To gather all the stars away from day.
Dawn brushes all the points of stars away
Unless they're folded in a cloud of dreams.
So, dream clouds drift and gather, starlight gleams
Until the days wax weary and grow gray,
Then tip and spill each precious hoarded ray …
Spill whole clouds full of stars in slanting beams.

This is my cloud, and still, I stand and hold
My eye upon its course, always, to seek
Fulfillment of dreamt dreams within its fold,
But I have heard the tongue of thunder speak,
And know, who longed for glowing fires of gold,
The cold damp feel of silver on my cheek.

Three in a Room

Three in a room … the other two and I,
The staff that women measure others by
Judges each one's shining, well groomed hair,
The matched perfection of each woman's wear,
And, having judged the things one cannot hide,
Attempts to measure height and depth inside.

You, Lilla, with the weary, wary eyes,
The swift and sullen movements as you rise,
You I need not measure anymore,
For you I've measured many times before.
Eve's lips must have held that bitter smile,
When, disillusioned in a little while,
She found the apple was no longer sweet.
I think her shoulders must have held defeat
As valiant, yet pathetic as yours do,
And then your eyes …
Yes, they I have seen through.
There have been women in so many lands
Who, hiding back of swords viewed bloody hands
With tragic eyes. Who, armed with swords of trust,
Have trampled thrones and nations into dust.
And in your eyes of sorrow, I have read
A weeping for someone … or something dead.

You, Mary with the softly shining hair,
The grave blue eyes and pleased, surprised, shy air.
In soft white wool you hold there, knitted, purled,
You've woven all the splendor of your world.
And I see your wide world as you love it,
Purity and peace, the splendor of it.
You I need not measure anymore
For you I've measured many times before.
Once a woman with a haloed head
Bent softly o'er a baby's manger bed.
In all this world, no woman was so brave.
I think her eyes must have been blue and grave.
And then I've seen you many times again
As you walked down a quiet country lane ...
When you wore bravely like a flag unfurled
Your love of God and sky and all the world.

Three in a room ... the other two and I.
The staff that women measure women by
Is done. And Lilla, standing up to go,
Sighs ... may she never know the things I know!
And Mary, standing, giving her a hand, thinks
They miss life who do not understand ...
It's strange how clearly all their thoughts I see,
Except, dear God, the way they measured me.

I Am Gypsy

I am Gypsy. I am fey.
I'm a pirate on the quay.
I'm the spirit of the sunset crimsoned tide,
And the surging, sounding sea
Is the pounding heart of me.
In every singing shell I there abide!

But you couldn't know,
No, you couldn't know,
For your eyes were foreign with blue blinding skies,
With a satin coated throng
At the harbor of Hong Kong ...
Or perhaps the thought of haunting, slanting eyes.

I am Gypsy. I am fey.
When the sea is stormy gray,
I pace the strand, stand pliant in the gale,
And my eyes, with dancing fire,
As the rising winds shrill higher,
Light the harbor for a ship of crimson sail.

But you couldn't know,
No, you couldn't know,
But when the sea is stormy, stormy gray,
And you set your sail to harbor
By the lighthouse of my eyes,
You will know that I am Gypsy. I am Fey.

———————

Bewitched

Come and buy my roses,
Blowing crimson roses,
Gallant gypsy roses
From a fairy's wall …
She, with eyes of dusky shadows
Twice as silent as the stillness,
Strange with queer, half-secret smiling …
Secret soul.

I remember, someone told me
She could charm the souls from people,
Weird them into elfin people
With her eyes …
Into beasts that ride the thunder,
Into mumble-dumb small people,
She could make the sun go down
And two moons rise.

Oh, she is mortal, mortal
'Til her eyes know shadow-laughter
Or still into a strangeness draw you
Ever close,
You, who thrilled at shadow-laughter.
In her eyes slow, sullen splendor
Is the sharp-thorned fascination
Of a rose.

I remember once I saw her.
She was talking to a shadow,
To the slim and straight small shadow
Of a child.
She turned and lightly touched me
With her chill white slender fingers,
And her touch was light, and, oh, her voice
Was mild ...

But in her eyes, the shadows
Were glowing, leaping, flaming.
They brightly blazed, receded
And were chill.
"You're a shadow, shadow, shadow ...
All the wide world is a shadow ...
Hence your thoughts will all be shadows,
And be still!"

So, I wander, vaguely wander,
Selling roses, crimson roses ...
Sell my gallant Gypsy roses
From a wall.
And my eyes are dusky shadows
And as silent as the stillness ...
Strange with queer, half-secret smiling,
Secret soul!

Wings of the Wind

Out of the darkening twilight comes the rush of the wings of the wind,
Through wheat fields of waving blue shadows and whistling 'round corners of stars.
On a hilltop a lonesome old coyote gives a wild cry for those of his kind,
And the wan moon peers through a cloud tangle, like a prisoner peering through bars.

My soul makes a shadow in corners and rides on the wind's beating wings.
It meets with the soul of the coyote … two wild souls, so free and untamed.
It hides in the wheat fields blue shadows and sings, and it laughs as it sings,
And the farm folk are startled at laughter, a mouthful of laughter unframed.

It laughs at the fatuous people who strive so to reach but their goal.
It laughs at the person they think me. They don't even know I've a soul.

*****Aola Seery, published at age 17,
Golden Harvest, Mistletoe Press, 1937*****

My Masterpiece

Oh, once I wrote a wondrous verse
And deemed it work of art
And vowed the world would kneel to hear
This product of my heart.
And the great would flock to touch my hand
For only the great could understand.

I sought out Lady Melody.
She smiled to see me there.
She sang her silver song to me
And shook her shining hair.
And the moon did dim
And the wind did cease
As she called my work
A masterpiece.

And then I searched and sought out truth,
All stern and white and cold.
He tore my hard-earned manuscript
With fingers cruel and old.
At the work I did
And loved so well
He laughed and called it
An empty shell.

I come to you in humbleness
And beg you hear me thru.
I thought these lines and rhymed these lines
And wrote them just for you.
Oh, my lines are crude,
But my soul finds peace
When a street lad sings
"My Masterpiece."

*****Aola Seery, published at age 17,*
*Golden Harvest, Mistletoe Press, 1937*****

Through the Centuries

Once in the very long ago
When all the world was young,
Up from a bit of barren earth
A bit of greenness flung
Its arms up to a starry sky ...
Now mind you this is true ...
And no one knew whence it had sprung
When all the world was new.

The green bit grew to be a tree,
And the world grew old in age.
The great tree died and turned to stone,
Dame Nature's printed page.
Now children come and count the rings
And wish that they had, too,
Been born the century of the sage
When all the world was new.

Once in the middling long ago
When the world was half-past old,
Here on this spot where I now stand
Men tunneled deep for gold.
A city grew in gaiety
And laughed its short life through.
Now crumbling wood and stone and mold
Mark the world that once was new.

And now the world is very old.
In the phantom city's shell
Dwell bats and mice and memories,
And the crumbling houses tell
A history just like the tree
To folks like you and me,
And the city lies, content to dwell
On when the world was new.

I hope that in the "sometime when"
When I have gone to be
Companion to the fallen town,
Companion to the tree,
Someone will find a thought of mine
Or a deed I chanced to do
And thankful be to one who lived
Back when the world was new.

*****Aola Seery, published at age 17,
Golden Harvest, Mistletoe Press, 1937*****

LOVE AND MARRIAGE

*Lola Aola Seery's Wedding to
William Palmer Vandergriff
July 11, 1942*

The Color of His Eyes

I loved a blue-eyed king, and he
A battle won for love of me.
And oh, his words were words of wonder …
Of battlegrounds and cannon's thunder.
I loved a blue-eyed king, and he
A battle won for love of me.

I loved a dark-eyed prince who gave
Me gifts of peace, my willing slave.
He spoke of drowsy amber noons,
And twilit hours, and crescent moons.
I loved a dark-eyed prince who gave
Me peace, and knelt, my willing slave.

I loved a ragged lad who came
From some far place he could not name.
He taught me battles sometimes cease,
And there is no such thing as peace.
I can't recall now, grown more wise …
What was the color of his eyes?

The Stranger

I lifted up my eyes and saw
A strange divinity. In awe
I heard him solemnly agree
To honor and to cherish me.
Those precious words I heard him say
And from his glory shrank away.

And when he turned, the ring to place
Upon my hand, I searched his face
For some small sign, but none he gave.
His mouth was stern. His face was grave,
But then he smiled the smile of you
With all your dear faults shining through.

My Sun, My Moon, My Stars

Though my life be all of brier,
And my roses all be dying,
And my moods be less than gladness,
And my voice be only sighing,
If your hand is in mine then life
Will be well worth the trying.
Betwixt us two, we shall come through,
Come through with colors flying.

Although I stumble over paths
Of stone with bleeding feet,
And know at every turning is
A new despair to meet,
Then still I'll hold my head on high
As I go, each to greet,
If you go forward at my side,
Then sorrow will be sweet.

Although the trail should grow so dim
That I should lose my way,
Though other idols crumble, fall,
And show their feet of clay ...
Although my life should know no light,
And all my skies be gray,
You'd be my sun ... my moon ... my stars ...
You'd be my night ... my day.

When Day Brings

When day brings to our little house
The routine tasks to do,
I find each dear, familiar thing
Gives back a bit of you.

The rose you set beside the door
Spills lovely, crimson bloom,
And all the dreams we planted then
Blow fragrance through the room.

Your hunting coat hangs in the hall.
I touch it as I pass,
Remembering crisp, autumn dawns
And opal-frosted grass.

Your wistful setter follows me,
His sad eyes asking "when?"
Deep in our hearts we both believe
You must be back again!

Cornerstone

If you would build a love and make it last
And hold against the storms you can't foresee,
Forget the you that you were in the past
And nevermore say I, but always we.

If giving up of self seems any loss,
If you would keep your own identity,
Then you will lose the gold and keep the dross.
Instead of one, you will be he and she.

An unshared sorrow is too great to bear,
Too great for two, God will not let it be.
In losing self, you only learn to share,
So, make it we, my child, so make it we.

Dream-Builder

I only helped you build, my dear,
A dream, or two, or three,
You, never dreaming dreams would die,
That some could never be.

You must be wary of your dreams
And shield them from the rain
And gird them well in armor bright
Against the lance of pain.

You must be chary of your dreams
Lest a bright diadem
Should blossom like a lovely rose
And die without a stem.

But since I cannot shield your heart,
I must make these dreams be,
And help you hold against the world
A dream … or two … or three …

Enough for Me

You talked for hours of your divine devotion.
In that oration, all that I could see
Were just three words you said as if you meant them,
And that, my love, is quite enough for me.

Dream Riches

Once I was rich with dreams.
A day and a day,
And I found I had given
My dear dreams away …

All but a little one,
A small one and lone,
Oh, a dark little dull dream
That never had shone.

I held it to the sun,
The wind and the mist,
To the rain and the starlight.
It turned amethyst.

I held it to my heart,
And it changed in hue
To the shade of a love-dream
That I knew for you.

Once I was rich with dreams,
And strange does it seem
That I'm now content to be
Rich with a dream.

On Her Wedding Day

I shall not weep. She would not have it so,
Though she is far away and would not know.
Tears should not fall upon a wedding day,
Though all is done and nothing left to say.
So, I must sit and think of other things ...
The way the kettle in the firelight sings,
Though all its song is aching loneliness.
She was an angel in her wedding dress.
She was so young. I sometimes wonder though
If I taught her all the things that she should know ...
That one should cook and sew as well as dream,
That woes are not as great as they would seem,
And that a woman's great gift is the art
To read in tired eyes a loving heart.
There's nothing left to say ... to say or do.
I must not weep. She would not want me to.
Beside the hearth her old gray kitten dozes ...
What shall I do with all these dying roses?

The Poet

He was as old as time and as young as time.
He spent long hours making two words rhyme.
Never twice the same were the things he said,
And he brought home roses instead of bread.
He stood in places where hills meet sky.
He said that laughter would never die.
So he left her laughter, and love, and his name,
And a ten-cent photo in a real gold frame.

But that's years past. When the neighbors went in
Today, they found where love had been.
Love had been, and now, long after,
Love lived on in remembered laughter.
They saw withered roses in place of bread
As they stood there silent in the house of dead,
And down where she lay who bore his name
Gazed a ten-cent photo in a real gold frame.

Second Helping

Morning passes,	I rush to take
And my day becomes a stew	The cloak of weariness you wear
Into which I stir	And hang it deep away.
Bitter herbs of frustration	My day is a golden bowl
Along with meatier portions of toil	In my cupped hands.
And a pinch or two of laughter	I offer it, and you
To make it palatable.	Drink deep and smile.
And then you	How blessed I am!
Come heavy-footed up the walk.	Two mornings in a single day!

To Know You Are There

To know you are there when the morning sun
  Comes out of the East like a golden cup,
To know you are there as the stars wink on
  And the moon like a sleepy child gets up,
To know you are there when the winds blow soft
  And the spring is here, and the year is fair;
    It is all that I need, and all that I ask
      To know you are there.

To know you are there when the ill wind blows
  And the fevers rise, and the earth is chill,
  And the winter walks with its wintry ways,
    And I am old, and tired, and ill.
When the trials come, and we need and want,
And it's more than a heart and a soul can bear,
  It is all that I need, and all that I ask,
    To know you are there.

To know you are there when the wind is still
  And the quiet trees let a lone leaf fall,
To turn to your thoughts and to meet your eyes,
  And smile with you at nothing at all.
When the dusk slips down like a silent shade
  To surround us both like a quiet prayer,
    It is all that I need, and all that I ask,
      To know you are there.

Compensation

Cupid by twin purple pools
Played with my heart. He let it roll
Into the depths. I followed fast
And seeking therein found a soul,

The goddess of the pool. To me,
The archer gave a swift, plumed dart.
"Because I love thee, Fool," laughed he,
"Here's compensation for thy heart."

*****Aola Seery, published at age 17,
Golden Harvest, Mistletoe Press, 1937*****

Tintype

Thirty years of Junes ago it was.
We looked at our wedding picture today,
And I was standing up, and Henry sat
Stiff as a board and held his hat
Against his chest as though his beard were gray,
And he was old as Father Time, himself.

Thirty years of golden Junes it's been.
The wedding picture faded just a mite.
My lace and frills and ribbons don't quite show
Like they did thirty years ago,
But still the dim old picture's quite a sight,
And dearer far than any miser's wealth.

Thirty years of Junes ago today,
The picture looked a little funny, too.
But Henry said, "Why, Mary, it's not queer,
And though it has been thirty year,
We haven't lost the romance that we knew.
The romance that we knew then isn't dead."

Thirty years of Junes ago this year,
Before we took the picture that you see,
I fell in love with Henry's helplessness.
That's why I married him, I guess.
The romance that we knew, Henry 'n me …
I laugh and kiss the bald spot on his head.

A Flower from A Bride's Bouquet

I am a holy thing.
I am a flower from a bride's bouquet.
I have lain against the heart of happiness,
Decked in lace and ferns and frills and satin ribbon.
When the minister had ceased his intonation
And the final words of tenderness were spoken,
I cast myself beneath her satin sandals
For her first step into this art of living.

Then, when the room was mute from echoed laughter,
And the room was dumb with all the silence, after,
There came one in the last dim shadows kneeling
Whose tears fell on my bruis'ed petals, healing.
I have cast myself beneath the feet of beauty.
Teardrops, like dew, have fallen on my petals.
All in the turning of a day … a day.
I am a flower from a bride's bouquet.
I am a holy thing.

Hearth Fire

There was a hearth fire long ago,
Just as there is tonight ...
A fire that shed a ruddy glow
Upon the room, and light
Reached one slim finger through the gloom
To lay a soft caress
On golden hair that filled the room
With light and loveliness.
There was a hearth fire long ago
In happy days that were,
But firelight, crowning silver hair,
Is so much lovelier.

Homecoming

Because I knew you would be tired
I put on this blue dress
And did not scold when you forgot
Your usual caress.

It's been a long time since you said
You loved me, loved me so,
But as I stroke your weary head,
I know, ah yes, I know.

The candles show a mellow light. A little while we'll sit and talk.
I lit them when I heard I'll put on my disguise
Your tired footsteps in the night Of admiration, dear, and try
And did not say a word. To not appear too wise.

Silences

As the frost's fine fragile tracery on glass,
As the transitory state of night and day,
This thing we know, yes, even this will pass
As all things else have come and passed away.

This flame will burn against our night and die,
And, so, these words we murmur here together,
And we must bow before it, you and I.
Only silences will last forever.

So, say no word to drown within this night
This solemn thing we know is not for saying.
God takes such times and makes them into stars,
And these will last as long as there is praying.

When You Are Away

Sometimes it seems a little strange
That when you are away from me,
That moons still light the quiet lanes,
That rivers still run to the sea.

That in the streets of little towns
There are the hush'ed murmurings
That speak of moments after eve,
And that somewhere a brown bird sings.

Sometimes it seems a little strange
That I should live, and I should move
Without the nearness of you here,
Without the dearness of your love.

But when we're walking side by side,
Together as the shadows fall,
I am content. I am all wise.
No single thing seems strange at all.

The Letter

I found it in my grandma's chest
Of things she'd treasured so,
A folded letter, sealed in wax
Three hundred years ago.

Her mother must have kept it safe,
And hers, too, kept untold
The secret that a letter held …
Three hundred long years old.

And I will keep the secret of
The letter never sent,
Oh, dark-eyed lady of my past,
And you may rest content.

The letter I shall leave unread.
Its words are not for me.
Three hundred years have had their way
With fate and destiny.

First Love

My hands were chill as melting snow.
The day was warm and sunny.
I laughed at an old joke
That wasn't very funny.

I cried when a bird sang,
And I still wonder why
That sadness made me smile,
And gladness made me sigh.

I waited for him all the day.
I wonder why I did,
And when he came at last …
I …
I ran away … and hid!

Words Unspoken

I read unspoken in your eyes
The words you wish to say.
Oh, keep them hidden in your heart,
Lest they should slip away.

Oh, hold them prisoned in your heart,
The words I dare not hear,
Lest all our world should fall apart
Upon my answer, dear.

It is enough, enough for me,
That in your heart there lies
A single loving thought of me
That's echoed in your eyes.

So, I shall reach my arms to you,
Eyes with tear mist glistening …
And should the words escape the heart …
Dear, I shan't be listening.

A Wishing Kiss

I looked long at a map today
And, oh, it is so far
Across the little painted squares
To that one where you are.

I breathed a single wishing kiss
Across the starry blue.
Unless it's tangled in the stars,
It should be reaching you!

Blue Dream

Oh, there are days when I have walked
On far blue hills with you,
When we have reached the crystal edge
Where nothing real is true …
That crystal realm against the sky
At night would touch a star.
By day white pigeons circle by
And gold-tipped daisies are,
And little winds that have kissed rain
Blow cool against the face,
And all things ache with loveliness
In that clear, sky-swept place.

And you and I against the blue
Have walked there hand in hand
'Til stars have dripped their scented dew
Across the shining sand,
And we have knelt at secret shrines
That none but lovers know
Who walk along these silver heights
Where only dreams can go!

Together

Man was not made to dream alone,
For dreams are for the sharing,
But what if there is no one near
For listening, or caring?
Then in the subtly scented night,
With slanting shadows sown,
One heart meets beauty's poignant blade,
And bleeds and breaks alone …
The lance of too much loveliness …
And falters there … alone.

But two … two walk the shadowed ways
And the gallant sword they wield
Is the bright, new beauty in themselves
To pierce the nights dark shield,
For beauty bends and beauty breaks,
And slays with her caress,
But beauty quails and hides her eyes
Before this loveliness …
This bright, new poignant point we've forged …
We, two … of loveliness.

Him Will I Love

Him will I love who comes to me
   With gentleness, and quietly,

Without a single word to say
   About his love which grows each day,

Who feels the bright, too poignant pain
   Of purple lilacs after rain,

But through his understanding great
   Is silent, inarticulate …

For my heart is a wing'ed bird,
   And it is frightened at a word.

New Lamps for Old

Do you remember, oh, my dear,
The songs we sang so long ago,
So sweet and low, so sweet and low,
When Spring was entering the year?

Now, when time's tale is almost told,
Do you remember, Love, the Spring,
Remember how we'd play and sing
"New lamps for old, new lamps for old!"

And how, in all those years we've changed,
And taken old lamps for the new,
And found our lives are thus arranged
In patterns fair and patterns true …

Old lamps have magic in their hold …
Old lamps for new, new lamps for old.

This Gift for Life's December

When we grow old, if you may still be near me
To share with me each simple, homely task,
To answer with your smile when you shall hear me …
This is the only gift that I shall ask.

If when the busy day is ended
We talk a bit of such things we know best …
"I wonder if they got the south fence mended?"
"Today I found a wild canary's nest!"

The clock will strike, and I shall ask you whether
You locked the door … did you put out the cat?
Then hand in hand, we'll climb the stairs together.
Dear Lord, I shall not pray for more than that!

Here Are My Dreams

Here are my dreams, Love … take them and hold them,
Bury them under the linden tree.
Take them and hold them, closely enfold them,
Keep them and treat them tenderly.

Some are of star shine, and some are of moon glow,
And one is the azure hem of day,
Some are snow crystals, and some are June glow …
Dreams to brighten a weary day.

Here are my dreams, love. I trust you to take them.
Care for each one and see how it gleams …
Yet, you question my vows as I make them.
Here is my answer … I gave you my dreams.

Promises

When I was young and the world was young, and life was for the living,
I told my love that the world was mine, and it was for my giving,
And I gave to my love my pledge, my heart, and I gave her a golden ring,
And my love, she smiled with a thoughtful smile, and she never said a thing.
Nay, she never said a thing.

And I older grew, and the world did, too, and oh, the time was fleeting,
And my rainbow always had two ends, and the two ends never meeting,
And I gave my love bread instead of cake, but I gave her a song to sing,
And my love, she smiled with a grateful smile, and she never said a thing.
Nay, she never said a thing.

So, the world grew old, and my dreams grew cold, and I was done with trying,
For I found my fortune come to me, and so there was no sighing.
For I gave my love love, and she gave love back. 'Tis a satisfyin' thing,
And my true love smiles with a loving smile, and she never says a thing.
Nay, she never says a thing!

The Bride

The organ, deeply humming, like a silent sea
Comes with a surging sound. My veil of scented mist
Sways as a leaf before its sudden poignancy.
This is no stolen meeting … is no laughing tryst.

And I, who have laughed, who have gone gay ways unthinking,
I, who have dreamed, but only the new dreams that are gay,
Who thought the cup of happiness was mine for drinking …
    I laugh now at this new desire that is to pray.

It is enough that I should stand quiet and still.
There is an altar there, there are tall candles gleaming.
I wonder if my presence before them would fill
The place with confusion. Or would I learn new dreaming?

I have no fear of altars. Have no fear, but to kneel
Before a sacred holy place without a reverence
Would be a sacrilege, but shaken, strange, I feel
A wakening to what is real. Omniscience.

And in the crystal mirrored wall, with shadows as a frame,
I see a tall white candle facing me,
Tall, and with a veil of mist, a veil of white pure flame,
Blowing with the breeze from the organ's surging sea.

An altar, and candles, and a new way of thinking,
And all in a minute or an hour of a day,
'Twixt a swift sun's rising, and swift sun's sinking,
And there is just a minute left to kneel and pray.

The time I have to wait is drawing to its close.
Shaken with my new dreams, I know that I must start.
But see, I have torn all the petals from a rose …
Its gay crimson cloak is gone, and there is its heart.

A Shield

Whenever I am angriest with you,
I bring the same old vision back anew ...
You, as you must have been when you were small,
A little boy with wide eyes seeing all
The beauty in this world of toppled thrones,
With all the precious faith that childhood owns.

I'm sure your boyish heart was haven for
The small lost dogs who sought a friendly shore.
Your pockets must have held a million things,
A mouse, a toad, some bread and jam ... kite strings.
The world today turns far too swift for one
Who knew the bright enchantment of the sun.

And there is space for disillusion's darts
When grown-ups keep a child's thoughts in their hearts.
So, when my heart is rent with hurt and pain,
And anger is a bright blade in my brain,
I sheathe again the sharp spear I can wield,
And stand between you and the world ... a shield.

———

Information

Ask me any question. You may ask me where
In the dimness of the forest sleeps the great black bear ...
Where in the meadow does the rabbit run ...
Where is the house of the moon and the sun ...
Where is my loved one ... and does he miss me there?
Ask me any questions. I can tell you where.

Ask me any question. You may ask me how
Do the field mice climb to the high hay mow ...
How do the birds know that winter's near ...
Ask me how much do I love you, dear ...
Ask me how the farmer knows when to plow.
Ask me any question. I can tell you how.

Ask me any question. I can tell you when ...
When it was that the world began ...
When all the fairies come out to play ...
When is the end of night, the dawning of day.
When shall I love you? From now until then.
Ask me any question ... I can tell you when.

Ask me any question ... anything but why.
Ask that of someone greater than I.
Why can't I answer? I just don't know!
Why do I miss you whenever you go?
Why do you make me smile and then make me cry?
Ask me any question ... anything but why!

Two Loves

One strand is very weak, but two will hold.
A little alloy always strengthens gold.
So, take two people and a wedding ring,
And you will have a strong and lovely thing.

A year is as a raindrop to the sea,
But fifty years can span eternity.
One love alone will last a single hour.
Two loves span a lifetime and will flower.

One heart alone is weak, will sometimes break.
One faith alone is small, will sometimes shake.
Two hearts, two faiths are like bread with its leaven,
To rise and rise and touch the gates of Heaven.

Reserve

They laughed at me	They tried in vain
Who spoke of love	To see within
As if I knew him well,	And dared to ask me why.
And so, I wept	"Your heart," they said,
Awhile and crept	"It seems so dead.
Into my hard, cold shell.	It was too young to die."

The gossips and	My heart is dead.
The tabby cats	They've buried it,
All try their best at tea	As everybody knows.
To pierce my shell	If they but knew
With things that tell,	My hard grey shell
Make live the heart of me.	Was lined with silk and rose.

***** Aola Seery, published at age 17,
Golden Harvest, Mistletoe Press, 1937*****

There is Such a Thing

You, and the sky, and a soft wind blowing,
Blowing in your lashes, and your tangled hair,
And I watching, and my love avowing,
At the sight, the delight of you standing there.

There is such a thing as love-and-dreaming,
Through today, or tomorrow, or yesterday.
The light of love through the dusk is gleaming,
Though star shine and moon glow all pass away.

What love is, there is no way of knowing,
But it must be something like a mountain high,
All mixed up with a soft wind blowing,
With a soft wind blowing and you and the sky.

Just That Way

Sometimes it happens just that way, you know.
Two pass and, pausing, meet each other's eyes,
And, in that brief moment, no disguise
Can veil the understanding, reaching so,

And drawing each to each, the undertow
Of all the years of precious dreams that rise,
When two pause, passing ... meet each other's eyes.
Sometimes it happens just that way, you know.

Yet, though I know that I cannot be free,
That from these ties which link us, I shan't stray,
I have no wish to put you far from me,
Though it be for a year, or for a day.
There is a word that names it ... destiny.
Sometimes, you know, it happens just that way.

When They Are Near

It's very nice to feel that Peter's near
On winter evenings when the fires burn low,
So quiet is his presence, and so dear,
But yet, I scarcely see him come and go.

But Colin, Colin sets a warming fire
That reaches to my very fingertips.
He taught me words like longing and desire
With every kiss he placed upon my lips.

I scarcely know when Peter comes and goes,
And Colin has a wealth of love to take,
But Peter's face in all my deep dreams glows.
It's Peter whom I weep for when I wake.

I Thee Endow

With all my worldly goods I thee endow ...
This moment's silver hush to hold and share,
The reverence in one small shining ring,
A cloak of beauty you will always wear
Before my eyes, the stars which burn and swing
Across bright lovely years, my dearest friend,
An ear to hear your laughter and your sighs,
And, as a night with trouble shadows ends,
A bright new hope to light the dawning skies.

With all my worldly goods, with all my faith
To hold the course the days trace through the years,
An arm of strength to ward away each wraith,
An understanding of the heart's swift tears.

With all my worldly goods, I thee endow,
And hill and stream and meadow anywhere
Will somehow seem, I know not why, nor how,
The lovelier because our love is there.
With all my worldly goods, I thee endow.

Prelude

I thought I loved you then. The moon was white
Behind the resting shadow of the trees,
And flowers were a fragrance in the night,
A barrier of shadows 'gainst the breeze.

I thought I loved you then, how very strange.
I think it must have been the night bird's call,
The twilight's murmur over sleeping hills,
That made me think that my poor love was all.

I thought I loved you then, but now, through tears,
I see a love I know I never knew.
The greatest love is never in the bloom,
But looking at life falling blossoms through.

———————

Mirror, Mirror

Mirror, mirror, let me see
The face of the one who best loves me.

I speak the words, and over my shoulder,
A little bit gray and a little bit older,
A little bit tired and much more wise,
A little more love light in your eyes,
I see your face by candlelight.
Oh, the time is short, and the change is slight
As again I whisper roguishly …

Mirror, mirror, let me see
The face of the one who best loves me.

Oh, many a thing has come to pass
Since first we met through the looking glass.
There at the foot of the cellar stair
I looked in the glass and you were there …
And many a dream's been dreamt in vain,
And many the heartache, and much the pain …
And still, I whisper so tenderly.

Mirror, mirror, let me see
The face of the one who best loves me.

———

My Life Had Need

My life had need of a sight of sea,
        The vast wild sea to complete it …
The sight of a sun-bright full-rigged ship
        Over the rim in a gliding dip
                As the sea comes up to meet it.
        Yet I never have seen the sea,
But a little wave's warm hand
        Comes reaching across the land
                To touch its fingers
        Against my heart.

My life had need of a sound of wind,
        With a tall tree to sing to …
Breathing its heart to a tall windmill,
        Clouds and sky, and a far-off hill,
                A world for a wind to cling to.
        Wind in trees I have not heard,
But over the prairie grass,
        A whispering seems to pass,
                Leaving a melody in my heart.

My life had need of so many things,
    Of a sea, and a wind, and you …
But now I know that my choice was wise.
    I've found my whole dream
        In your eyes,
    And lovelier far than I knew.
        Yes, now I have seen the sea,
Heard wind in trees above me,
        And knowledge that you love me
           Is sea, and a melody
                To my heart.

A Valentine

It's a bit of lace and paper, but perhaps, dear, it will do
The thing that I'm a-wanting, that I'm hoping for it to.
Perhaps this bit of paper with its lace and gilt will say,
"Oh, I'm sorry, sorry, darlin', that we quarreled yesterday,
And I'll never, never, never say the things I said again."
You broke my heart, my dear one, but I'm sending in its place
This substitute of paper … of paper and of lace.

The sun's behind the hills now, and it is stormy weather,
But think of all our dreams, dear, the ones we've dreamed together …
How when the sun had gone to rest and twilight filled the skies,
We'd look across a baby's curls into each other's eyes,
And how when night had slipped away and hours of darkness done,
We'd wake a tiny little house in time to greet the sun.
Remember all our dreams, dear, and try to find a trace
Of dreams to bring back dreaming, in this paper heart and lace.

It's just a bit of paper, but it's sent to let you know
That black is white, and white is black, if you, dear, say 'tis so.
Hot is cold and cold is hot, and here, my sweet, is there …
You may be right and may be wrong, but darling, I don't care
As long as love is always love, and you are always you,
And near again, and you and I make one instead of two.
It's a bit of lace and paper. Do you 'spose, dear, it will do
The thing that I'm a-wanting and I'm hoping it will do?

Effervescence

I saw a diamond lying on a leaf,
And I plucked it, dear, and brought it home to you,
But the sun shone gay, and the diamond ran away.
How was I to know 'twas only dew?
I heard a fairy laughing in a brook.
Such a silver laugh, a merry sounding fey,
So, I brought a cupful of the brook, dear, home to you,
But the laughter disappeared along the way.

I saw the lovelight shining in your eyes.
My thoughts stole moonbeams from the sky, so did they soar.
Cruel words brought them hurtling from their heights to lie,
Moonsilvered in the shadows on the floor.
The woodvine's leaves are sparkling with the dew.
The brook-fey sings her lilting song as sweet,
But I am dumb to sight and sound … nor can they lift
My heart from disillusion's shadow at my feet.

**** *(Aola Seery, published at age 17,*
Golden Harvest, Mistletoe Press, 1937)****

FATHERS, MOTHERS AND CHILDREN

*Aola with her first-born daughter
Lola Jacquelyn Vandergriff -1943*

A Name

Mother is the newest name,
　The newest name I know.
I weave it in the words I say,
　In every stitch I sew.

I hear it in the sound of tears,
　I hear it in the laughters.
It stands between me and the world.
　It's blazoned on the rafters.

Oh, I shall hear it often, yes,
　Too many times, too many ...
But what if it had happened so
　I hadn't heard it any?

It stands in softest pinks and blues
　Between me and the wall.
I had not known this little house
　Was quite so beautiful.

Yes, it is in the words I say,
　In every stitch I sew.
Mother dear ... the newest name,
　The sweetest name I know.

Grapevine Swing

Do you remember the days in September,
The blue days, the crisp days, the haze on the plain,
The leaves on the scrub oaks all flaunting bright colors,
Maze yellow and red through the September rain;
How we trudged so slowly that dusty brown roadway,
To the old-fashioned school as we heard the bell ring,
And how our thoughts wandered to where the brook blundered,
And we longingly thought of the old grapevine swing?

I haven't forgotten the first day of autumn,
The road to the schoolhouse that casually curled
Like a dusty brown ribbon between the tall hedges
That set the small pathway apart from the world.
I also remember how often we wandered
From the path to the school as we heard the bell ring,
How often we hurried to where the brook scurried,
How often we turned to the old grapevine swing.

*****Aola Seery, published at age 17,
Golden Harvest, Mistletoe Press, 1937*****

Mud Pies

I see that you have learned at six
A grown-up lady's bag of tricks,
As you gaze with complacent eyes
At rows and rows of small mud pies.

You've crimped the edges, oh, just so,
And they present a charming show,
And so do you before your store
With handprints on your pinafore.

You're very young to be so wise,
To learn the witchery in pies.
Someday when you're grown up, baby,
You'll recall your youth, and maybe

Prince Charming will come riding where
You are and take the kitchen chair
In that corner where it's cozy
And watch you working, flushed and rosy.

Don't look so dubious, my dear …
Just wait until that time is here.
Cross your bridge when you come to it.
Win your prince … oh, you can do it.

Those freckles brown will disappear.
What matter if they don't, my dear …
Your youthful art you can employ
And make a pie for Billy Boy.

Lessons in Kite Flying

Tommy wants me to come out
And fly a kite upon the hill,
But I can only sit and pout.
I'm very busy being still.

No matter how I'd like to go …
Tommy don't know how to fly it,
But I must watch it flying low,
And keep right on at being quiet.

There's our canary in his cage.
I'm sorta sorry for that bird!
It puts me in an awful rage
To have to sit … not say a word.

Someday, when I am grown-up, maybe,
All big and stout and six feet tall,
Then I will prove I'm not a baby …
I guess someday I'll show 'em all.

First I'll let that canary fly
Away and wing with all his might.
Then I'll climb that there hill and show
Old Tommy how to fly that kite.

Five

Just one times five's my little boy,
And all my laughter, all my joy,
And all my pain and all my tears
Are bound in one, by five short years.

Too soon, he will be five times two
And I'll remember how he grew
So many inches since today,
And growing taller, grew away.

When he has grown to five times four
I cannot dream then anymore,
For suddenly, I'll look and there
I'll see a stranger, in despair.

And then he will be five times three.
I'll not believe it when I see
He is as tall as I at last.
I'll keep these years and hold them fast.

Then he will smile, and I will see
A younger lad of five times three,
Of five times two, of five times one,
My little Son! My little Son!

Heartbreak at Six

In vain are all your nods and smiles,
Your feminine, though infant wiles.
In vain are all your gusty sighs,
Your tempting rows of small mud pies…
For what are beauty, cooking art,
To hold a young man's wandering heart?

You wonder what you haven't got
That he deserts you on the spot.
You count your freckles, one by one,
And lose the count before you're done.
Glamour ... humph ... it's all a yarn.
The young man doesn't give a darn!

But save your tears, my princess fair,
And you will find that he does care.
It's 'cause that girl next door is new.
Oh, someday he'll come back to you.
So, smile and make those mud pies still.
It always has worked ... always will!

My Goblin Child

Hello, Little-Girl-With-A-Dirty-Face,
Wrinkled dress and bedraggled lace,
Tumbled hair like a golden crown,
And one sock up and one sock down.

I'm looking for my little girl,
All crisp and clean with hair a-curl ...
And stockings turned down, oh, just so,
And a lacy dress as white as snow.

Instead, I find here in my yard
A little goblin, smudged and scarred.
The fairies must have come, I fear,
To take my child and leave theirs here.

Alas for curls that hung just so,
For lace and ribbons white as snow,
For dainty stockings and the rest,
But I love my goblin child the best!

Stormy

Oh, we're due for stormy weather.
In the Heavens, not a feather,
Not a wisp of cloud is stirring
In the sky.
The old gray cat is purring
As he tries to be assuring,
But the baby has his face all
Fixed to cry.

Yes, we're due for lots of thunder,
And the neighbors all will wonder
If there's any peace of mind that
Can be had.
And I'm sure they decided
Just about as soon as I did
That he had a disposition
Like his dad!

Yes, we're due for lots of raining
From the blue, though nothing's paining.
There's mutiny and lightning
In those eyes.
Before the day is ended,
All the dewdrops will be blended
In a rainbow that will promise
Clearer skies.

Mother

She's as silly as me, and a prize-winning "goop."
She's a pain in my neck, and she's flies in my soup.
She's always a-whistlin' or dancin' a jig
'Cause she's twice as Irish as Pat Murphy's pig.

She makes me so mad, just so mad I could die
When she scolds me for slowness. Were I meant to fly
They'd have given me feathers instead of big feet.
Come to think of it tho', she's pretty darn sweet.

Of all of the people she is the worst tease.
She can think of more tricks than a houn' dog has fleas.
Be mad when she reads this? You're mistaken, not she.
She'll invent something meaner to do to poor me.

She's sweet to me sometimes (whenever I'm sick).
And sure she's a sap, that darned Irish mick.
She a blarneyin' smoothie and the bane of my life,
But I guess that my dad picked a mighty fine wife.

***** Aola Seery, published at age 17,
Golden Harvest, Mistletoe Press, 1937*****

Coffee Break

Sonny's off to school, and now
        Mother breathes a happy sigh.
She's searched for pencils high and low,
        And hunted, frantic, for his tie;

And, too, she wiped up all the ink
        That Sonny spilled upon the floor,
And put new laces in his shoes,
        And found his hat behind the door,

And now, she pauses here to breathe
        At almost nine o'clock.
A towel is on the front room floor,
        And there's a dirty sock.

The breakfast dishes yet to do.
        The flies begin to hover.
A rivulet of cream pours forth
        And down the table cover.

Yet Mother breathes a happy sigh
        That the whole room echoes, too.
Sonny's off to school, and now
        There's nothing much to do.

Pockets

I say the magic words, and lo,
I place my hand in here,
This dark recess, and draw forth things
That are most wondrous queer.

Comes first of all, a bit of string,
A piece of bread and 'lasses,
A toad that wags a feeble head
As through my hand it passes;

A nail, a key, a rusty screw,
All these I find, and more
The pen I lost a week ago,
An ancient apple core.

I am a great magician, yes,
These things I find are all
From a tiny little pocket
In a small boy's over-all.

And, as I find a furry mouse,
A little one, and dead,
And place it on the heap beside
The 'lasses and the bread,

I say the magic words again …
"I love him." I regret it,
But I must add a little prayer …
"Oh, let me not forget it."

Elmiry

Elmiry was a cross old maid
Who couldn't stand a kid,
And when we saw her coming,
We always ran and hid.
But who bound up my finger?
Cross old Elmiry did.

The Kelleys over cross the tracks
Had not a thing to eat.
Then I saw old Elmiry
A-goin' down the street.
She left a basket at the door.
Did those kids have a treat!

Elmiry was a cross old maid
Who never laughed or cried.
She held a person in contempt
Who stole a thing or lied.
Who would have guessed we'd miss her
When she died?

*****Aola Seery*, published at age 17,
*Golden Harvest, Mistletoe Press, 1937*****

Prodigy

When she was just a little girl,
A prodigy audacious,
She gazed upon the moon as cheese
With appetite voracious.

And then when she was sweet sixteen,
The neighbors 'round about
All set their watches at the time
She and the moon came out.

Now she looks forward to the time
The wan moon ends each day,
For only when the moon is high,
She puts her work away.

Wisdom

As a child I used to know
More than grown-ups ... told them so.
Knew the earth was flat and wide
With China on the other side.
That stars were pointed, as a rule
Like on my chart in Sunday school.
That I would wed a princess fair
(When I grew up) with golden hair.

When to man's estate I grew,
More than the old ones still I knew.
I'd wed a princess fair and proud,
A dream which vanished like a cloud.
For all I know, the earth is square,
For I have not been everywhere ...
And stars have points for all I see.
They wound me with their poignancy.
And as I watch the young ones grow,
The more I age, the less I know.

Tiptoe Time

It's tiptoe time in the little house.
Baby is sleeping, is sleeping again,
After a trip to the shadowed vale,
After a night in the arms of pain.

It's tiptoe time in the little house.
The dawn comes up like a rosy wraith,
And Mother is sleeping beside the crib,
And holding fast to a mother's faith.

It's tiptoe time in the little house,
As a tired man draws a tired breath.
For he and the woman, hand in hand,
Have fought all night and won 'gainst Death.

Fiddle-Footed Cowpoke

I'm a fiddle-footed cowpoke
And I'm ridin' high
With my seat in the saddle
And my hat in the sky ...
I'm on terms of speakin'

With my saddle's creakin',
And the yucca's bloomin'
Lookin' almost human ...
And when it rains
Then quicker than sooner

There's the track of a boomer,
Or a snake with a rattle,
Or misstrayed off cattle,
And I holler, "HI"
To the peopled plains.

Fairy Grandmas

Are you a fairy?
Well, so am I.
Let's put on our wings,
And gaily fly
To the moon and back
And up and down
From Laughterville
To Happytown.

We'll stop the clock
And turn back time.
No one will know
I'm nine times nine
And you are three,
Nor ask us why.
Are you a fairy?
Well … so am I!

Close to the Stars

Baby's there in his tall highchair
As dusk steals o'er the land,
With his wee head bowed on the highchair tray,
And a spoon clasped in his hand,
For he is as sure as windows were
Made for stars to peep in
That a tall highchair, and a tipped blue bowl
Were made for a child to sleep in.

A daffodil on a high, high hill,
That is our baby's hair.
A kingly throne for a kingly king,
This is his tall highchair.
And the blue tipped bowl is a bit of sky.
So, he sleeps at the end of day,
One hand clasping a silver star.
One dipped in the Milky Way.

Following a Star

It's his first Christmas, and my prayer
Is to Thee ... Mary, Mother.
Through His child's laughter, you and I
Know kinship with each other.
You must have smiled, as I smile now,
When, from the manger's hay,
His wee hand pointed out his star
In laughing childish play.
You must have smiled as I smile now,
So mother-fond to see,
My baby reaching toward a star
On his first Christmas tree.
This is my prayer ... I feel so near
To you, although afar ...
Let my child know the glory found
In following a star.

Featherstitched In Blue

I have fashioned little dreams,
Featherstitched in blue.
I've stitched a life with silken thread
For you, my son, for you.

And all inside a little room
Where lovely visions are,
Each window has a rainbow veil,
Each window frames a star.

I have set every lamp aglow.
Each mist-veiled star is gleaming.
The low wind sings a lullaby,
And I, I still sit dreaming

And stitch a life in silken thread
For you, my son, for you,
And make a mother's lovely dream
All featherstitched in blue.

Dream-Shiner-Upper

I shall, when I'm grown-up
And ag'ed tomorrow,
Be a Dream-Shiner-Upper,
A Laugher-At-Sorrow,
Or perhaps a Sweet-Smiler,
Or Wish-Chaser-After,
And gild over woes with
Remembering laughter.
A Frown-Smoother-Over
I'll be when I'm old,
A Rainbow's-End-Searcher,
And find that the gold
Is a Happiness-Treasure,
And that will be pay
Enough when I'm ag'ed,
Day after Today.

Lost Mother

Mister, see if you can find her.
Honest, next time I will mind her.
I turned around and looked to see
A dog, and she got lost from me,
And now I don't know where she is.
Do I feel awful ... oh, gee whiz!

I knew I should have held her tight,
But it was right in broad daylight.
It happened right before I knew it ...
Then it was too late to do it,
And here I stood, and she was there,
And then she wasn't anywhere!

Go on and tell me I've been bad.
Don't mind scoldin'. I'd be glad,
'Cause I deserve it. Go ahead!
Golly, I wish I was dead.
A fella don't mind bein' bossed
When he's got his mother lost.

Ma!

Ma, I've lost my feet!
I was sure that they were on
When I waded in the water,
But now, oh, gosh, they're gone!

When I waded in the water,
I was sure that they were there,
But the water got all muddy.
Can't find 'em anywhere.

Ma! I've lost my feet!
You'd better run get Pa.
Ouch! What's that? A crawdad!
Ma-a-a, I've found 'em! Ma-a-a!

How Much I Envy You

The baby has grown up and gone away …
And there is his little shoe,
And you who gilded and set it there …
How much I envy you.

For this little shoe is a fairy ship
That will take you back again
To the tear wet cheeks and the clinging arms
Of a baby … after pain.

Oh, this little shoe is a magic thing
That will take you back to stay
When you never dreamed that a blue-eyed babe
Would grow … and go away.

Milady

I kneel beside Milady's chair,
And kiss Milady's feet.
I praise milady to the world.
Milady is so sweet.

I dress Milady in her robes
And comb Milady's hair
'Til it frames her face in shining gold.
Milady is so fair.

I gave Milady all my heart,
But it's an even trade.
I am Milady's mother, but
I'm still Milady's maid.

***** Aola Seery, published at age 17,
Golden Harvest, Mistletoe Press, 1937*****

Tiger, Tiger

Stealthily stalking the woodland path,
Thinking like tigers and walking like deer,
Small boys go a-hunting, and no twig breaks.
The lordliest lion goes limp with fear
As
they
draw
near.

Watching at windows, the women wait,
Thinking like mothers, and dreading the sound
As a shell's ricochet marks a bird's fate,
The blood of a squirrel stains the ground.

While they are conquering woodland paths,
In faraway jungles, and for their sakes,
Thinking like tigers, and walking like deer,
Big boys go a-hunting
And
no
twig
breaks.

Mother-Fond

What is the tenderest, laughingest thing
That a mother's eyes can see?
A gay little frock on a sleepy head,
With the back where the front should be.

What does she know that's beautiful?
What does she know that's gay?
A gay little frock on a pastel lawn
On a perfumed April day.

But oh, inexpressibly beautiful,
And oh, ineffably sweet,
When a smudged little frock has been folded away,
And baby is fast asleep.

———

Love Triangle

We love you dearly, she and I ...
But she has eyes as blue as sky,
While mine are dark ... though you have told
Me that they're lovely. She has gold
To wear as halo for her head,
Though dark hair's pretty, as you've said.
But what's a poor tired wife to do,
I saw that young girl kissing you!
And what's more, dear, I suppose
You've told her she's a pretty nose.
I heard, as plainly as can be,
You call her pet names you've called me.
In fact, I don't know what I'd do
If she were not so much like you ...
And weren't we so very glad
When the first word that she said was Dad!

Schoolyard

Across the grade schoolyard a paper blows,
And I wonder if the wild wind knows
These ABCs were written by a hand
That could someday wisely rule this land,
And for his own museum chose to wedge
It safe from reach beneath a thorny hedge.

Refugees

There is a vast and silent sea
That women cross alone
That other little lives may be …
A sea you've never known.

There is a shore the other side,
Of shadowed vale and hill
Where all who've touched, but Death, have died,
But touch, you never will.

For never will you reach your hand
Across that stretch of sea
To one who waits upon the strand,
The child that cannot be.

But yet there is another sea,
More tangible, and there
Death touches house and man and tree …
His dark hand everywhere.

And on that stricken shore there waits,
Where battle rages wild,
Bound in by tears and fears and hates,
A frightened lonely child.

Oh, woman, woman, reach your hand,
And reach your heart out, too,
For Mary, Mother of our Lord,
Looks down and blesses you.

To Michael

A world of words, as yet unsaid,
Belongs to this young sleepy head,
    Young Michael.

His blue, sweet eyes to see are seeming
Dreams that yet await their dreaming,
   Dreams of things that are to be,
   Great visions that we cannot see
    For Michael.

What gifts he brings, we cannot know,
Must rest, content to watch him grow,
    This Michael.

He may set his country's flag unfurled
   In some new unfamiliar world,
   May set new stars against the sky,
   May teach the eagle how to fly,
    May Michael.

But now he chooses but to sleep,
Rose petal hands curled 'gainst his cheek …
    Our Michael.

And as he lies, so dreaming there,
   A sunbeam tangles in his hair.
   His dreaming of the yet-to-be
   Is ended as he smiles on me.
    Ah, Michael!

Why

My wee one came to me and asked
With eager eyes alight,
"Oh, Mummy, can you tell me, please,
Why is a white horse white?"

I stopped, and pondered on this thing,
And answered, "This is true.
White horses are so white, my dear,
Because they're never blue.

"White horses are pure white because
Red roses are so sweet,
And autumn leaves blow in the wind,
And people have two feet.

"White horses are so white because
They grow that way, I've heard,
And a thing on wing that's not a bug
Is usually a bird;

"The fragrance of the prairie wheat
Wafts on the autumn breeze,
And elephants eat peanuts ...
And monkeys live in trees!"

My wee one went upstairs to bed,
And in her prayers that night,
She said, "Please, God, tell Mums an' me,
Why is a white horse white?"

———————

In This Room

My little son,
The shades are drawn, and there has been
A fever in this room, and death was here.
I heard his voice in the scraping of a twig
Against the windowpane.
Death was here and now is gone,
Leaving nothing but a quiet hush
And the small sound of your breathing
As you breathe evenly again.

Death has gone. And I, who have never been away,
Am come home again.
I have been looking beyond your little face
Too long ... too long.
My eyes have been fixed upon far horizons,
The edges of worlds, the places where ships
Slip off into the skies and disappear.

I have been sick with the longing of the sea,
The sound of it, and the smell of it.
I have strained my eyes with watching for a sail.
My mouth has longed for the feel of strange words to say,
But now, my ship,
The ship with its sails set toward the white moon of the sea,
Whose sails know a tint of crimson from a Red Sea moon,
Has come to harbor in this little room
Where the shades are drawn, and Death has been.
The white moon has gone down into the sea.
The Red Moon has gone down into the sea.

There was a time when my longing was to build ...
Before Death came and went ...
I was looking beyond your little face
To towers against the sky.
I was going to build of mortar and of stone
These dreams of mine, to pierce the clouds on high,
To write my name upon the cornerstone
Of all the world… my name in lasting stone.
But yesterday, when Death had come and not yet gone away,
And all was numb, I found a thing to do
In putting scattered blocks away,
Thinking perhaps you might not need them more.
I thought of all the times that I
Had scattered all your toys, unthinkingly,
Had toppled dreams more wonderful than mine.

But now, my dream
Of building all is centered in this room
Where the shades are drawn, and death has been.
My palaces are ashes in the dust.
My senseless towers trampled in the dust.

———

No Less a King

He bows his head and, weary, wends him home,
    Walking tired and work-worn into peace.
    A working man he is, and honest, rough,
    Untrained, unused to riches, or to ease.
He wends him home. A crude unpainted shack
He calls a house, but through the windows, light
    Sends out a shaft of welcome for his eye
And guides his last tired footsteps through the night.

    Inside, he spreads his gnarled hands to fire.
    The children bring his slippers, smiling up
    Into his face, then last his old wife comes.
    She bears with her hands the magic cup,
    A cup of steaming liquid … fragrant, brown …
With peace and health and warmth filled to the brim.
    She pauses by the king of this poor house,
    And smilingly presents her gift to him.

    Of all the kings who live in palaces,
    Of all the kings who rule on land or sea …
    Of all the kings who find peace at their firesides,
    Of all these kings, no less a king is he.

The Old Ways

I'm very old and a little queer,
And I hold the old ways very dear,
The old, old things, and the old, old ways
Of the old, old times, and the happy days.
I name the stockings and pin them on
The mantel piece. There's one for John,
And one for Mary, and one for Dan ...
I remember well how they laughed and ran
And I stood back for the kiss they'd give ...
And one for the baby who didn't live.

I guess I'm old and a little queer,
But I've fixed the tree as I have each year.
I see in the light of the star set high,
A ghost of the children of days gone by.
John with his bright and serious face,
And tousled hair brushed into place,
And Mary with braided chestnut hair,
And little Dan in the doorway there
That led to the room where Baby lay
Still fast asleep on a Christmas day.

I wish them health and Christmas cheer,
And they go away for another year ...
The ghosts of my children when they were small,
And the baby who never grew at all.
But I tiptoe past the nursery door,
Crooning a lullaby once more.
I'm very old and a little queer,
And I hold the old ways very dear ...
The old, old things, and the old, old ways
Of the old, old times, and the happy days.

Wee Know-Nothing-Curly-Head

Wee Know-Nothing-Curly-Head
Must leave her downy little bed
And take her books and march away,
For she must go to school today.

And that is why I shall not see
The sun from nine to half-past-three,
Nor hear the things the fairies said
To my Know-Nothing-Curly-Head.

And that is why I shall not know
What breezes whisper when they blow,
Nor hear a baby robin cry,
Nor see the queen a-passing by.

I must hold fast to all these things ...
The memory of gauzy wings,
The fairy ring beneath a tree ...
These things she has brought back to me.

And she will go to school today
And find her world is made of clay.
The dreams she built about a star
Will vanish in the things that are.

'Til someday thoughts of things that were,
Through a baby's eyes will come to her,
And through the veil of As-They-Seem,
She'll find again the power to dream.

Wee Know-Nothing-Curly-Head
Must leave her downy little bed,
And take her books, and march away ...
For she must go to school today.

Moon Madness

A witch put a curse on the moon last night,
And the Death-Wind whistled in the eerie gloom,
And I hid my head in the dull half-light
When the witch put a curse on the moon.

A witch put a curse on the moon last night.
When wind was forgotten and the night was still
'Til a grim ghost wolf from the prairie days
Called his gaunt ghost mate to the kill.

Mother came with a lamp and her sweet, brave eyes,
And away went the strange half gloom,
And the witch hid her eyes from the glow of love
And flew away home on her broom.

Lullaby Lady

Oh, what shall we do, oh, what shall we do?
The sun in the sky is swift dying.
The lullaby lady has fallen asleep,
And all of the babies are crying.

The stupid old sandman has spilled all his sand,
And tired little eyes are all teary.
The dolls have all fallen and broken their heads.
Oh, hushaby, darling, my deary.

See, Baby, the sky is all studded with stars,
Though everything else has gone wrong.
The sandman will gather the sand that he spilled,
And Baby will sleep before long.

Oh, what shall we do, oh, what shall be do?
The sun in the sky is swift dying.
The lullaby lady was out late last night,
And all of the babies are crying.

*****Aola Seery, published at age 17,
Golden Harvest, Mistletoe Press, 1937*****

Catalpa School, First Grade

Turn, our teacher says,
And I obey. Two eyes, two ears
Atop a quivering stalk of eagerness,
The smallest child in school.
The air is thick with chalk dust
And the smell
Of hard-boiled eggs in lard pails
Brought from home,
The redolence of barnyards
From the shoes
Of those who must do chores,
The scent of books,
Perfume of knowledge to
A six-year-old.

Rise. With trembling knees
I stand. Ahead of me
Beyond the teacher's desk,
Bright countries lie

Aswim in copen seas.
And in my hand, The Book,
The Book of Words, to learn and link
Into a magic chain
To hang my life upon.

Pass. With solemn step
The first grade moves toward the front
Past all the desks
And past the centered stove
To make an ordered row
Before the Maker of Our Miracles.
"Open up your books," she says,
And it begins.
Page one...

*****Dedicated to Aola's first grade teacher, Dorothy. Written in the 1980s*****

Madonna in a Blue Gown

Madonna in a blue gown smiling down
Where a small child wrapped in slumber, silent lies ...
A blessing on thy bowed and haloed head,
The beauty in thy love brimmed, shadowed eyes.

There was a night when shepherds, leaving sheep
To seek a star that hung o'er Bethlehem town,
Found a wee babe in a stable, fast asleep ...
Madonna in a blue gown, smiling down.

But that was long ago. No less a light
Illuminates this picture of today,
For still the Wise Men follow stars through night,
And bear their gifts of love, so old ones say.

A room ... a cradle rocks. No stable this.
A slender girl. She might be Mary, too.
She smiles above a new babe, slumber-wrapped ...
Madonna in a faded gown of blue.

The Fiddler

He carved his fiddle from a flowering tree,
And took for the strings a fairy's laugh,
And a springtime sound, and the sound of the sea,
And the strange deep sound of the storm-God's wrath,
And he made sweet music, wild and sweet,
Music for fleet feet to dance to,
'Til the gay notes slowing on the swift upbeat
Turned to low, slow heart songs to romance to.

He played 'til fairies crept from curled-up leaves
Into the light of the noonday sun,
And all of the stars came out to hear,
And the shy moon laughed and joined the fun,
And the moon came out and joined the sun,
And oh, it was such lovely weather,
And the boy who hated girls, and the girl who hated boys
Heard and smiled and danced together.

Then he played again, and how he played,
Low, slow songs for Death to sing,
Songs of love and songs of woe,
Of a broken heart, of a broken wing.
Oh, he played, and his songs were light and gay,
Then he played and his songs were sad and deep.
Then he touched his fiddle with the bow of life
And hushed a cross little, tired little child to sleep.

The Drum

Ta Da Rum! Ta Da Rum! Ta Da Rum A Dum Dum!
Somebody gave Baby a little red drum.
About the house, 'round the house, all of the day,
Boom Ti Boom! Boom Ti Boom! Learning to play.

While the Heavens resounded with spurious thunder,
And neighbors surrounded in curious wonder.
I took from my baby his little red drum.
Ta Da Rum! Ta Da Rum! Ta Da Rum A Dum Dum!

With a "Bing, Sir, you're dead!" and a "Bang, Sir, you're dead!"
Somebody gave Baby a gun, and he fled
To find all his playmates, the people he knows,
"Bang, Sir! You're dead now!" He laid them in rows.

His old pal advanced in true canine glory,
Bombed with tomatoes, sanguine and gory.
Where did Baby get all these things in his head?
Every "Bing, Sir, you're dead!" Every "Bang, Sir, you're dead!"

Ta Da Rum, Ta Da Rum, Ta Da Rum a Dum Dum!
I gave back to Baby his little red drum.
I put up the gun, and the drum said to me,
"This is the home of the brave and the free,

"Of the Star-Spangled Banner ... long may it wave
O'er the home of the free, and the home of the brave,"
All to the tune of a little red drum,
Ta Da Rum, Ta Da Rum, Ta Da Rum A Dum Dum!

To a Teenage Son

I stir throughout the night at every sound
Of tires on pavement wet with snow or rain.
I flinch with every flickering of light
As passing cars illuminate my pane.
I wonder if, someday when you are far
And I am old, and life's begun to wane,
If I will see, in every passing car,
Your lights turn in the drive again …
Your lights turn in the drive again …
Your lights turn in the drive again …

Quilts

Grandma painted pictures of the fancies that she built.
Her paintbrush was a needle. Her canvas was a quilt.
Grandma was an artist, but there's poetry and prose
In the "Nine Patch" and "Winding Blades,"
"The Tulip and the Rose."

Then there's the "Jacob's Ladder,"
And I can't recall one's name.
Oh yes, now I remember, it's called the "Irish Chain."
I love to watch her stitching and bending o'er the frame,
Bending o'er "Dove in a Window"
Or "The Wedding Ring."

Grandma paints her pictures, and her tiny stitches show
The love and care and tenderness her children know.
Her "Flower Gardens" lovely, but the one that you should see
Is the one called "Duck and Ducklings"
She finished just for me.

*****Dedicated to Aola's Grandmother, Mrs. O.O. Seery;
Aola Seery, published at age 17,
Golden Harvest, Mistletoe Press, 1937*****

Little, Dirty, Ragged Urchin

Little, dirty, ragged urchin
Tryin' not t' cry.
Think yer tough an' grown-up, don' cha…
Well, Sir, so am I!

Think that yer a big, bad fella!
Think that you won't go with me!
Well, yer Daddy said t'gitcha,
An' yer goin' with me, see?

An' yer Daddy said t' tell ya
That he had t' go away …
That he ain't in jail no more. Y'see,
He's gone upstate t' stay

With a pal o' his called Peter
Where the gates ain't locked, he said …
Oh, God, how do ya tell a little
Kid his daddy's dead?

There musta been some good in him,
No matter what he did,
To have such trust and lovin' faith
From such a little kid!

A single switch was pulled. It took
His life … all that he had.
I gotta tell a little kid
What happened to his dad!

Well, Son … we'd best be goin'.
Think yer tough, huh? So am I!
Little, dirty, ragged urchin…
Tryin' not t' cry!

*****On her 1940s radio program, Aola explained this poem: "…These are the words of a friend of a man who was sentenced to death…"*****

Somebody's Spoiled the Baby

Somebody's spoiled the baby,
And I'm wondering who.
Somebody rocked him whenever he cried,
And sang him a lullaby, too.
Somebody's spoiled the baby,
And everyone's blaming the other,
But the one who rocked him whenever he cried,
That was the baby's mother.

Somebody's spoiled the baby.
Daddy tossed him up high
And gave him his watch to play with
And tried to feed him pie,
And Grandma hung about the crib
To watch her little man
And gave him all the love she had …
The way a grandma can.

Yes, somebody's spoiled the baby,
And I'm wondering who.
I might have done it … then again …
Again … perhaps 'twas you!

School Days

Down the path with pails a-swing,
A little queen … a little king …
Through the meadow, past the brook,
Dropping here and there a book,
They go to learn to wisely rule …
My little king and queen, to school.

And I remember as they start
The way that they have ruled my heart …
The way that I have bent the knee
Before their awesome majesty.
Too small a kingdom was their first,
Now they must rule the universe.

Down the merry path they go
That my feet took so long ago.
I see in misty changing scenes
A horde of little kings and queens.
A tiny kingdom's best to rule.
Time teaches that in Life's great school.

This Is the Day

This is the day, and I must climb the stairs
As I have climbed them wearily before,
To take the schoolbooks from their box
Beside the door, recalling once again my dark despair
In putting them away.
This is the day.

This is the day.
And I must trace again his faded name,
And sharpen all his pencils for him, too.
The lunch pail I will fill as I was wont to do.
And scan the autumn skies for sight of rain,
His eager feet to stay.
This is the day.

This is the day,
And neatly stacked again beside the door,
The speller and the reader wait his hand.
I close my eyes, and pray in vain, for here I stand
Remembering that he will come no more
With good-bye kiss, and say
This is the day ...

———————

Christmas, 1967

I gave you, son, at the hour of your birth,
    The things I inherited, too,
And that's why you think that man on this earth
    Can do the things God does not do,
That fighting alone makes nations kneel down,
    And that man must live by the sword.
Someone walked barefoot in a thorn crown
    And did all these things with a word.

So, now I am searching for some small thing,
    A flower I pressed in a book,
To send you out armed with, some tender thought,
    And I thank God, a smiling look.
For, if I can give you these little things …
    And the kingdom is made of such …
Then this heritage from the old, cruel kings
    May not, after all, mean so much.

Borne on the Wind

That night the wind went howling,
And horror shapes went prowling,
And the moon hung weird and sickly
In the gloom.

A sad shape, wan and weepingly,
Came on the wild wind seeking me,
With tales that fortunes lay in shadows
On the moon.

The wind inland was throbbing,
And I beseeching, sobbing,
Begged for just a portion of the fortune
On the moon,

But the shape laughed at my wailing
And on the wind went sailing,
His misty mantle trailing
Like a plume.

***** Aola Seery, published at age 17,
Golden Harvest, Mistletoe Press, 1937*****

Of Kingdoms

This is a child's kingdom,
His knowledge that in each and every flower
A tiny singing spirit dwells,
That little leaves are set asway
By unseen hands, and footprints left at dawn
In dew among the grasses and the reeds
Lead through enchanted moments all the day,
A whispered sound upon the vagrant breeze,
A message on a petal as it falls.
These are his meeting with the fairy world
Where he is king.

This is a grown-up's kingdom,
A tiny singing spirit, but more real,
Small hands that can be seen, small hands, which hold
All that there is of magic and miracles.
There are small feet to follow all the day,
And when the night comes down, and all is still,
The real and unreal melt into the dusk.
This is the time when kingdom's totter, fall,
When a sleepy little child must close his eyes,
And the grown-up kneels beside,
His willing slave.

A Cradle Rocking

Poor little child … you who are doomed to know
No mother's smile or gentle love-dimmed eyes,
No father's rough affectionate caress,
No soft, sweet note of love-sung lullabies.
Poor little babe, for whom cruel life has set
In all this world no bit of love apart.
Your childish laughter makes my eyes grow wet,
And sets a cradle rocking in my heart.

Your lullaby will be of sorrow, ever.
Your love shall come of strangers such as I,
A love grown out of sympathy and pity,
Yet your laughter, childish laughter, knows no cry,
But there shall come a day when worlds grow smaller,
And young men shall be old, and babes be men,
And there will be no one to point the pathway …
Oh, little child … will you be laughing then?

Who Tends a Tree

There was someone had a tree and didn't love it.
I watched it blossoming and saw it bear.
Its branches bowed beneath the weight of fruitage.
Somebody watched them break and didn't care.

There was someone had a child and didn't love it.
As bends a weighted bough, I saw him grow.
A burdened branch must reach a time of breaking.
Somebody saw him break and didn't know.

There was someone rich who didn't know of loving.
I, who am poor, and through my poverty am weak,
Know strange, rough feel of bark against my fingers,
The touch of baby hair against my cheek.

In everything that grows there is a lesson.
He harvests best who prunes and tends a tree,
And to a child, if he would harvest blessing,
Gives of his love, his strength ... says lean on me.

Father-Mother

I have faith in a power that is higher than I,
And I've done all the things I should do ...
And now I must be ... or at least I must try ...
Their father and mother, too.

And I must keep faith that is shining in eyes
Through the veil of a child's blessed tears,
And I must be brave through each sun's set and rise ...
Through all of the lonely years.

I've told them the sunshine is Mother's sweet face.
God give me strength that I may explain
If they should ask why, when the clouds take its place,
For tears are so like the rain.

And I must do the task that is given to me,
And be faithful to it and be true,
Or at least I must try, for now I must be
Their father and mother, too.

Lullaby

Hush, for the evening is deepening softly.
Hush, for the earth has grown fragrant and still.
Long shadows are cradled in earth's gentle hollows,
The sun leaves a kiss of goodnight on the hill,
And here you are weeping, when dusk in her velvets
Has hung you a star on a tree's highest bough.
Then why are you weeping? Because you can't reach it?
Because the wide world's so much greater than thou?

Because the world's greater, your tears are as dewdrops
In a great river that runs to the sea,
But a star, just for you, is affixed to a treetop.
There's someone, so tender, who watches o'er thee.
So hush, for the evening is deepening softly
And long are the shadows that lie on the land,
And you will find someone to reach the star for thee
And put the star, shining, in your eager hand.

———————

What to Name the Baby

What to name the baby? He should have a name
That some great man has had before, and that will bring him fame.
The name of some great president should grace our little son …
Of Roosevelt, of Lincoln, or perhaps of Washington.
But, oh, 'twould be a heavy crown for our wee babe to wear …
'Twould sit all topsy-turvy on his curly golden hair.

What to name the baby? Why, someday he might grow
To be a musician … artist … or poet, don't you know?
And since through all his life he should with one name be content,
Why, we should give him one that would express his temperament,
And Percival, or Lancelot, he might go somewhere with,
But they somehow lose their music when they're added on to Smith.

What to name the baby? His hands that cling to me
Will someday rule the whole wide world and mold its destiny.
From continent to continent will spread my baby's fame,
And reverent lips will praise him and will speak my baby's name …
Not Roosevelt, or Lincoln … no, nor even Algernon.
I wonder, do you think, dear, that, maybe … the name … John?

Mother's China Plate

Mother had a china plate
As blue as blue can be,
Blue as the heavens overhead,
Blue as the eyes of thee.

And patterned on this china plate,
This plate of gorgeous hue,
Was a china lass who looked like me
And a lad who looked like you.

This happy pair were always meant …
Oh, it's as clear as fate …
To live in blue, blue china bliss
On Mother's china plate.

"It's fun to live on china plates
In blue, blue china bliss,"
Said the blue-plate lass to the blue-plate lad
And threw a china kiss.

"It is," he said with hop and skip,
And sorry to relate,
A great crack ran from side to side
Through mother's china plate.

But with a little pot of paste
We were able to restore
The blue-plate lass to her china lad,
Restored forevermore.

If but our loves and friendships, too,
That we break in clumsy haste,
Could be mended so by loving friends,
Friends with a pot of paste.

"When was blue plate half so gay
Or lassie half so fair?"
Asked the lad as he plucked a china bloom
To twine in the blue girl's hair.

The blue boy smiled a china smile
And begged a china date.
So, they went to tea at the blue tea shop
On mother's china plate.

*****Aola Seery, published at age 17,
Golden Harvest, Mistletoe Press, 1937*****

Farewell

Here I stand and, oh, the house
Seems so empty … strangely empty … with him gone.
It seems like yesterday … right there he stood,
With his new shoes and his Sunday manners on.
I remember how he'd come right through that door,
Searching for a little bite to eat,
And I'd scold him hard for tracking up the floor …
Make him go outside again and wipe his feet.
Oh, I scolded him. If mothers only knew
What I know now, as here I stand in tears,
They'd love the prints of little smudgy hands
And sort of overlook those dirty ears.
It seems like yesterday. Right there he stood,
With his new shoes and his Sunday manners on,
And I stand here, in tears and, oh, the house
Seems so empty … strangely empty with him gone.
It wasn't death that blinded me with tears,
It wasn't death, but it was just another
Farewell kiss from such a little boy
Grown up big and taller than his mother.

Heritage of Hills – Class of 1939

With the passing of the Pioneer, his spirit did not die.
Ours is the heritage of hills ... the heritage of hills and sky.
As we pause upon the threshold, seeing new trails stretch away,
We look again to old trails that we loved so yesterday,
But the travelers are ready for the work that must be done ...
Feet steady on the path of life and faces to the sun.

We stand between realities of tears and joys we've met
And the curtain, which in parting shows us life in silhouette,
And still, in indecision, we would lift a hand to stay
The passing of the morn of life into the clouded day,
But dimming in the distance are the trails that we are shown.

Who will take this trail together?
Who must walk that trail alone?

We stand upon the threshold, and we pause to say goodbye.
The trails of preparation we have followed, you and I,
Will take us through the darkness and will lead us to the light,
Though the trails are all uncharted and are blanketed in night.
So, head held high, remember ... we cannot, shall not fail.
Life turns to us and beckons us. Forward! Down the trail!

Forward ... one step forward on the shifting sands of life,
And echoed from the future comes the sound of tears and strife ...
But thunders speak a challenge as the echoes roll and die ...
"Yours is the heritage of hills ... the heritage of hills and sky!"
There are new worlds to conquer ... new fields for you to till!

This is your life ... now take it! Take it! Make it what you will!

**** Written for Aola's high school graduation and read again on her radio program the following year and dedicated to her brother, Jimmy, for his graduation. ****

TOIL AND PERSEVERANCE

Rancher's Son, Bill, 1939

Shadows

They say that she sees shadows
Of folk who aren't there
And walks and talks with shadows
Though she cannot leave her chair.
She lives back in the long ago
When things to her were dear,
When love it was, and time was not,
So, folks all call her queer.

She sees the shades of Indians,
Of a cabin on a claim,
The shades of three fine brawny sons
Who in the earth were lain.
Now in the winter of her life
She recalls that which was sweet,
The fragrance of the prairie grass,
The sun on golden wheat.

You may stand by and talk to her,
But still you can't pierce through
The myriad woven shadows
That shelter her from you.
I think that in the judgment, when
She's rewarded for her lot,
God will let her keep the time love was …
Love was and time was not.

***** Aola Seery, published at age 17,
Golden Harvest, Mistletoe Press, 1937*****

While Others Sleep

Death's bones clatter in the wires,
Ice laden, moaning, crackling wires
That swing and touch and burn against the sky,
A single flame, and Storm is master here.
He rages back and forth, his post to keep
'Gainst tiny man, who, armed with stick for spear,
And coil of wire, and such, approaches near,
For service must go on
While others sleep.

Death's voice chatters in the wires,
The spitting, whining, screaming wires,
The dancing wires, confederates of Storm.
All ye who deep in peaceful slumber lie and
Think that light is lasting, light is cheap …
Know ye that in the icy storm men try
To hold the singing wires against the sky.
For light means life to some
While others sleep.

Oklahoma Father

No still quiescent hands, no silvered hair,
No gentle eyes that fill with tenderness,
For here there is no place for gentleness
In bleak blue eyes that pierce the dust-filled air.
His hands are clenched against the world though care
Has marked his brow with lines of weariness.
Against the seething storms of strain and stress,
He has a cloak of power and faith to wear.
He leans against a wailing amber wind,
His darkening brow with perspiration dewed,
And when the crop is in, the cotton ginned,
And there are walls about him and his brood,
And all is done, and all the harvest binned,
With rough hard hands he gives his children food.

Winter Respite

I love the plains and the open sky
And the far, faint hills between,
The snow that sifts into downy drifts,
White as a shroud, and clean,
When a man can rest from the harvesting,
And dream of another plowing,
While the window ledges gather snow,
And trees in the storm stand bowing ...

When a man can rest from the harvesting,
With nothing much left to do,
But the few chores left in the morning chill,
And those in the evening, too,
And the outside pump is frozen tight
Against our vain endeavor,
But the fire on the hearth is blazing high,
And the wood will last forever.

Yes, I love the plains and the open sky,
And the far, faint hills between,
When the pain and the toil is repaid in joy,
As the snow falls ... calm, serene.
In the evening, I sit beside the fire
And read the age-old story
And know that the footprints I have made
Are blanketed in glory.

A Farm Woman's Diary

The sky was cobalt blue today,
Of such a gorgeous hue today,
Of just the shade for love.
I saw myself 'neath arching trees,
Tall and swayed by gentle breeze,
Resting, watching at my east
The skies above.

Instead, I baked eight loaves of bread,
And turned and hemmed a dress instead,
And patched and aired the featherbed …
The commonplace,
But in between, I did my hair,
And ironed a faded dress to wear,
And put some powder with great care
Upon my face.

I took the eggs and went to town
And sold them, in my faded gown,
And hid my discontented frown …
They did not see.
A townsman to me bowed his head.
"To me you're beautiful," he said.
"I envy much the man you wed,"
And so said he.

And then he shook my work-worn hand,
So scarred and stained from touch of land.
I've lost my discontentment and
Perhaps I'll rest
Tomorrow 'neath a sky of blue
If I've no other work to do,
And watch the sunset's rosy hue
Fade in the west.

———————

Ladder of Life

There's a ladder made of sifted dreams,
That leads to love and happiness.
It leads where few stars cast their beams,
This ladder of success.
The muses made it by sifting dreams …
Drifting dreams …
A gay mirage, not what it seems
To those who follow its transient gleams,
And then, the kindly muses put
Friends to steady it at the foot.

And, oh, I would be a helping hand
To steady the ladder that leads to fame.
Here at the foot I would ever stand
With an unknown face and an unsung name.
Dear God, success I don't demand …
A lauding band …
Applauding hand …
But just to aid some climber and
Steady a ladder in shifting sand,
For I somehow feel that, should I stop
To assist at the foot, I shall reach the top.

*****Written at the age of 15*****

Sing Me a Love Song

Sing me a love song,
Not of romance,
But of work and clothes to mend,
Of a floor to sweep, and a child to rock
In the twilight at day's end.

Sing me a love song,
Not of glamour,
But of gray days and blue skies,
Of pain and laughter and toil. Reward …
One smile from your dear eyes.

Four Ages

Up, Man, the earth calls, and you must to your plowing.
Sadness will not stay thy task, nor joy, nor death, nor birth.
So up Man, and out Man, although your head be bowing.
You'll half forget your troubles in the fragrance of the earth.

Up, Man, the earth calls, and you must to your sowing.
The dews are fallen on the leaf and are near gone away.
So, sick Man or well Man, the planting days are going,
And you must out and seed the soil the dawning of this day.

Up, Man, the earth calls, and you must to your reaping.
The earth has turned from green to gold, all since the seeds were sown.
The heat, Man, is sweet, Man, though sun high up is creeping,
And weariness is welcome when one brings the harvest home.

Instead of seven ages, you, Man, have but four.
First you sow and then you reap and gather in the grain.
Then it's rest, Man, in peace, Man, though winds howl at your door.
God will buy your crop of love … pay double for your pain.

***** Aola Seery, published at age 17,
Golden Harvest, Mistletoe Press, 1937*****

Retirement

I have been warned that when I reach the shore
Where riptides end and sea and sand are kind,
I'll long again to struggle in the depths
And strive to win against the waves and wind.
Shall I find nothing in the shallows then?
Will languor not be healing to my soul?
Survival in mid-oceans raging storm
Permits no lull to heal or become whole.
I shall reach that shore triumphantly
And, gazing at the riptide's surging foam,
Will know, here as a child I stood, yet I have been
There all the way and have come safely home.

Her Hands

To learn to love a person, you must see
Her hands, for they are marked by soul and thought.
What miracles have blunt, hard fingers wrought,
And work worn hands can fold so reverently
In fervent prayer and touch Eternity.
The weary hands, the poor hands that have fought
More than their share of sun. No mystery
Is this to me, yet you taught me wonder
That you could bring, with fingers slim and white
Peace to fevered brows, or take some blunder
Someone has made and set it all a-right.
And then, of pastry strips, a whole crust under,
Make of a pie a poem and a delight.

Wings for Her Feet

If I were but a fairy child with misty gauzy wings,
I'd drink the silver cup of song Dawn scatters with the dew,
And I would learn the melody the hush'ed night wind sings,
And whisper it to ears that have no song to listen to.

If I were but a fairy child, I'd cease arranging clouds
Against the freshened morning to be painted by the sun,
But I would put a beauty in a cobweb's lacy shrouds
For sick eyes that must lie and watch the work which should be done.

If I were but a fairy child, I'd plant a single flower
In a woman's every footstep to spread its fragrance sweet,
To gladden every tiring task and crown each weary hour.
I would fashion fairy sandals to put wings on tired feet.

Her 'n' Me

Her 'n' me built this house,
'N' it's bin a long time ago.
Back in them days
A board house like this
Was a rarity.
I seen the time when we never knowed
If we'd see the morror's sun or not.
Injins!

They'd pass by them black jacks
And hit that thin place there
And sorter disappear-like,
Through the woods the other side
Of the pasture.
They never stopped though,
And when they's gone,
Her 'n' me would grab each other
And dance, we'd feel so free.

Her 'n' me and this house
Started out together,
And we seen a lot …
Good times an' bad,
But lookin' back,
The good times look awful good,
And the bad times not half so bad.
Times like settin' 'round the fireplace,
Winter nights, and the time little Alf
Fell in the sorghum.

Her 'n' me and the house
Started out together,
And then, fastern the winter snows,
First thing we knowd,
It was her 'n' me
And nine boys and two gals.
Three of them boys we lost,
Before they's more'n waist-high,
And time has took the rest
An' scattered them to the four winds.

Woman's World

Just a little hut is all I ask
That stands 'gainst the rain and the night,
That stands like a haven against the blast,
With a hearth that is clean and bright,
With Mollie a-tending
The hearth, and mending
Of clothes by the fire's soft light.

Just a little hut is all I ask
With a love that can warm it through,
And an old clay pipe, and my glass of ale,
And two dear sweet eyes of blue,
Of Mollie a-smilin',
The sweet hours whiling
At the tasks she is wont to do.

Then she lays her sewing and such aside,
And, tired from the homely tasks,
She makes her wishes and dreams her dreams
And puts on a lady's mask.
But a tight door shut
In a wee warm hut
And Mollie are all I ask.

Futility

He climbed the hill and stood with folded arms
And bare brown sturdy legs spread wide apart,
With grave, proud mien, as of some small child king
Who gazed upon the land that held his heart.

Those sun-browned curls ... he needs no other crown,
His head held high in flower fragrant air ...
Do you know, Boy-With-Curls-All-Tumbling-Down,
Of all the kingdoms, yours is far most fair.

The valley lands are pretty, it is true.
In crazy patterns sprawled below they lie.
The in-between is pretty, too, but you,
You think in terms of high fields and of sky.

You stand, a king, against white clouds and blue.
Wildflowers spring in places where you've trod
To greet the one who climbed to this high field
To plow his furrow next to sky and God.

And others sit and watch
And sigh to see,
And say that life is just
Futility.

———

HOME AND HOLIDAYS

*Aola and Bill's first Christmas
San Antonio, Texas, 1943*

The Beckoning Light

A lantern on the door of a little white house,
Broken it is, and dim,
With a few panes out, but the light shines forth,
And beckons my footsteps in.

The walls will be old and gray, I know,
And the corners will dusty be,
But the heart that lives in a little white house
Is calling. It calls to me.

So, I shall go to the little white house
And scour the corners clean
And scold at a lonely old gray mouse
And paint a few chairs green.

The Gypsies who live beyond the hill
I'll forget I ever knew,
And I'll mend the lantern and shine it 'til
It sends its glow to you.

Declining an Invitation to Dinner

Thank you so much for asking me,
I'd really love to stay,
But a little house is calling
A hundred miles away.

I'll miss your scented orchids,
The music and the wine,
I'll miss the quiet service
And the mellow candle shine.

But in the little house that waits
I'll tie a baby's bib
And put a kettle on the fire,
And broil a juicy rib!

I'll smile at the adored one
Who provides my daily bread
And bow my head in rich content
While grace is being said!

Star Wishes

When the star had led the wise men
To where the Christ child lay,
An Angel wrapped it in a cloud
And packed it deep away.

But this year they unpacked it
For its work was not yet done,
And they made it into wishes
And they named each point for one.

First, I wish you wisdom, glory
And the pearl of greatest wealth,
The one more precious than the other,
The God-given gift of health.

They gave me them and told me
To find one kind and true,
To give them to a loving friend,
So, I send them, dear, to you.

I wish you friendship and the gift
To smile your tears away
And that God may send you
happiness
Upon this Christmas Day.

*****Aola Seery, published at age 17,
Golden Harvest, Mistletoe Press, 1937*****

A Little House

Oh, we will build a little house the little hills between,
Where the sun will rise at dawning and will touch it with a dream.

Oh, we will cast a silver net into the blue, blue day,
And catch a rosy tinted cloud and ride in it away

Across a rosy tinted world, and when we come home late,
Oh, won't the people look to see a pink cloud at the gate!

Oh, we will build a little house between the little hills
Where twilight plays a violin of muted whip-poor-wills.

Remembering Wee Homes

I listened to the little sounds
I've heard so many eves,
The north wind promenading
Through a corridor of trees,

The footsteps of remembrance,
I heard them rise and fall,
Heard ghosts caught in the cobwebs
In the dim and dusty hall.

I listened to the little sounds,
I did, and hear them still …
Remember, though I've left the place …
I do, and always will.

Why didn't someone say before
Ghosts grew from year to year,
And leaking roofs and drafty rooms
And such could grow so dear?

You, who this house will serve as home,
This house by rich forgot,
Remember, though you leave the place,
Wee homes hold such a lot.

You, Who Lived Here

Though we've never met, I know you
So much better than you'd think,
For you left your kitchen dirty
And a ring around the sink.

The parlor floor was dusted,
And the bedroom rather clear,
But the back steps, and the closets,
And the corners, oh, my dear!

But you left a fairy story
Lying in the dusty hall,
And you planted Gypsy roses
On an old, neglected wall,

And your papered walls are bright and gay
With cabbages of pink.
Though we've never met, I know you
So much better than you think.

Interior Decorating

It is such a little house, so little, but my dear,
There are fairy prisms fastened to a crystal chandelier.

There aren't many chairs and things to fill the space within,
But love will gather in these walls and fill them to the brim.

There no one waits to welcome, but a gaunt, gray mouse …
But we shall throw the front door wide. It's such a lovely house.

Fences

I like a fence that leans
To greet you as you pass,
Tip-a-toe in dandelions
And tall striped grass,

Hanging on loose hinges,
A slattern growing older
But wearing wreathes of roses,
Spring, off the shoulder.

My fence is a spinster.
No climbing vine can hide
The rigidity of spirit,
Stiff, unbending pride.

Virtuous, though Spring-clad,
Closely latched her door,
She marches down the boundary,
Iron to the core.

Next time we build our fences
We'll know what we're about.
Some builders build to keep love in.
Some build to keep it out.

An Empty Heart

I always wake with such a hope
Upon an Easter day.
It almost seems that he is there,
Has never been away.

Perhaps, as one so long ago
On Easter day did rise,
So comes my little dancing child
With laughter brimming eyes,

With eyes of childish tenderness,
With eyes that fill with fun …
What else could turn night into day
And light again the sun?

But when the night comes down again,
My lad once more I lose,
Save an empty Easter basket,
Save an empty pair of shoes.

The Shepherd

Following the star of eternal faith
Not bearing gifts of frankincense and gold
Nor myrrh, my king, for riches I have none
Save for the fifty woolly sheep within my fold.
I come to thee.

God's Angel came in the dead of night
Saying, "Rise up ye shepherds. Go to Bethlehem.
There you will find the babe newborn
With the Virgin Mary, and you will give to them
This prophecy:

This tiny babe wrapped in swaddling clothes
For my sons' sins shall suffer on the cross.
He will be my sons' salvation, and at his death
The world will mourn in sorrow at its loss
On bended knee.

*****Aola Seery, published at age 17,
Golden Harvest, Mistletoe Press, 1937*****

My House

This is my house. I see it every morning
When the dawn is trying all the windows
And in the evening
As it draws the twilight close and, with it, peace.
I have furnished it with dreams and laughter.
There is so much can be done with tender dreaming
In a little house,
Such a little house,
A white house, sleeping on a hill.

This is my house. I can hear every morning
Childish laughter waking to the dawn-song,
And in the evening,
When the twilight steals along the hill with peace,
And soft sweet sound of lullabies and laughter,
My sweet dream fades away. I wander onward
To my own house,
Lonely old house,
The big house on another hill.

Home

I cleaned the kitchen cupboard, and I swept the kitchen floor.
I polished up the doorknobs, and I swept behind the door.
I dusted in the parlor, and I moved things round about,
And found, though cleanliness moved in, I'd swept the home-ness out.
So, I took the sofa cushions, and I threw them here and there,
And I scattered books and papers with a very careless air.
I spilled powder on the bureau,
Tracked from the yard some loam.
Then the children all came in from school …
"We're so glad to be home."

Ghost House

Pathetic little house of broken windows,
Sometimes I pity you, I do, and yet
I know your lonely rooms are trod and haunted,
Made less lonely by the ghosts you can't forget.

Ghostly grandmas set the rockers creaking,
And babies long since shadows silent cry.
Sliding footsteps echo, never sleeping,
Vibrations of a soul too strong to die.

And you have known the laughter of the living.
You've heard them laugh, you have, and helped them weep.
You gave them shelter, gloried in the giving,
And now you guard your ghosts, content to sleep.

Should houses have a God and have a heaven
You'd pass before the scrapers of the sky,
Rewarded by immortal life unending
Because real life had never passed you by.

*****Aola Seery, published at age 17,
Golden Harvest, Mistletoe Press, 1937*****

Sacrilege

They bought the place and moved down from the city.
They shaved the lawn to make it pretty
And built a great stone house of many rooms,
All dark and chill, and silent as the tombs.
They tore the home place down, from earth to rafter,
And sought to fill a place like that with laughter.

They let the hired man go. He left next day.
He was too rough and rustic, and then they
Sent back and got a dandy from the town
To fill the place of that gross country clown.
They sold old Tom and Jerry off the farm,
And put their fancy horses in the barn.

They stayed there but a time too short to measure,
Then moved back to the city and their pleasure.
The house squats dark and silent on the land
That she and I had chosen, hand in hand.
The land, unplowed, untended, skyward rolls.
Oh God, why must we poor ones sell our souls!

Ever Since I Came

I'm, oh, so glad you came to call.
Neighbors should be neighborly.
I've waited ever since I came
For you to come and call on me.

But no one came except your hens
To scratch in plants that I set out.
Your Junior slapped my Mary Jane
And woke the baby with his shout.

Then Junior broke my windowpane
And tied a tin can to the pup.
You radioed 'til one o'clock
And kept my poor, tired husband up.

The scent of all the things you cook
Comes drifting over here to me.
The day that you had cabbage, all
My friends were here for tea.

Oh, no, you mustn't leave so soon …
Neighbors should be neighborly.
I've waited ever since I came
For you to come and call on me.

Thanksgiving

What is there to be thankful for
On this Thanksgiving Day?
Perhaps the thought that I can kneel
Whene'er I wish to pray.

I'm thankful for the things I see,
The things that God has blessed,
The sun that rises at the dawn …
At evening sinks to rest.

I'm thankful for the things I hear,
That bird songs do not cease …
The melody a soft wind weaves
From harp strings of the trees.

And then I'm glad, so very glad
That I am who I am.
My song is one of freedom … peace …
I am American.

For what I see and what I hear
And for this life I'm living,
I clasp my hands and bow my head,
Today is my Thanksgiving.

The Star

I must be up and busy, for the year
Turns gay with holly and with mistletoe.
I must dust all my dreams of long ago
And hang them high to warm me with their cheer.

Oh, time turns tinsel tawdry. I hold dear
A sparkling skein of silver song to glow
When all the tides of time have ceased to flow.
When baubles break, I shall hold my dreams near.

My Christmas tree, set in the window there,
I'll drape with old dead dreams that live again,
Old dreams that have been polished with a prayer,
With tinsel still untarnished from the rain,

And, oh, the star of love my tree will wear,
Undimmed by time, undimmed by tears ... by pain.

Dear Santa

I guess that you will be surprised to see,
From one who scorned you in his later youth,
This letter from a grown up ... this urgent, anxious plea,
Asking for gifts of love, of love and hope and truth.

Take away my envy and my greed.
Give me the gift of loving simpler things.
Too many of life's bon bons disagreed
With the boy who loved the sticky candy canes.

But that small boy's so very far away.
The pass is blocked with sins and hates and sneers.
I doubt if even Santa and his sleigh
Can ever cross the ice of fifty years.

*****Aola Seery, published at age 17,
Golden Harvest, Mistletoe Press, 1937*****

A Crooked Christmas Tree

I bought a crooked Christmas tree
When I was down in town,
And knew its silver shining star
Would be a rakish crown.

Yet in my mind, I saw afar
The little twisted pine
Wrestling winds to sight a star
Above the timberline.

And though the star is set aslant
It does not shine the less…
The tree's soft branches bowing down,
Our few small gifts to bless.

———————

A Tree in a Trailer Window

For this, we thank Thee reverently,
This littlest, bittiest Christmas tree …
Just room for a candle and a star,
A bit of tinsel and ten cent snow,
But, oh, the star's light reaches far
And warms us with its glow.
Just one red candle and angel hair …
But there is more than Christmas there.

A bit of tinsel and ten cent snow …
All for Christmas, and none for show.
One small window made more bright
For a star that the wise men may have seen
Sends out a million points of light
From the tip of the tiniest evergreen,
And there is a radiance of cheer
Which says there is more than Christmas here.

Here is peace from the great world's din,
For light and love do dwell within,
And standing here in the winter night
We can see the ghosts of the wise men go
With their gifts of love up the pathway bright,
Where the small star shines in a tender glow
From the littlest, bittiest Christmas tree.
For this we thank Thee reverently.

One Candle

The Christmas lights were lighted
As I went down to town
On a bleak December evening
As the sun went down.

The Christmas lights were lighted
And the town was full of cheer.
Laughter from a child's heart
Is a good thing to hear.

The Christmas lights were lighted,
All the hearts were full of joys,
But I am too old now
For laughter and noise.

I bought a tallow candle,
Red wax, and tall,
Just one tallow candle,
And that was all.

I climbed up a high hill,
Over it and down.
Gone were the Christmas lights
From down in the town.

The Christmas star was lighted.
Something was there
Like God's voice speaking
Through the wind's soft prayer.

I listened to a music
As the star hung low
And placed my tall candle
In the white drift snow.

And then, from the Heavens,
A light came down,
More than all the Christmas lights
Down in the town,

More than all the Christmas lights
In the marketplace.
The skies grew away,
And I saw God's face.

I bought a tallow candle,
Red wax, and tall.
Just one tallow candle,
That
    was
        all.

Faith

A star hung over Bethlehem
And lit the shepherd's way for them,
Made a path of life for the sons of Shem
Upon the sod.

There is a light for us today
Nearer, yet farther from where the child lay
Which, if we knew it, would light our way
Home to God.

*****Aola Seery, published at age 17,
Golden Harvest, Mistletoe Press, 1937*****

The Tiniest Evergreen

The tip of the tiniest evergreen
Lifted its head from a stunted clump
Of weeds that grew like an oasis
On the very edge of the city dump.
It raised its head, and stood up tall,
And seeing what was to be seen,
Bowed its head, and grew quite small …
The tiniest evergreen.

For a sluggish river flowed beside …
Dark as the mouth of Hell …
And this was the scene at Christmastide
On which the moonlight fell.
From the gaping door of a sagging shack
A lame child watched the scene,
And the moon sought out, in the night's deep black,
The tiniest evergreen.

The moon dripped silver from its boughs,
And the lame child stood to see,
And slim and straight, with outstretched hand,
Walked to his Christmas tree.
To another child who bore a cross
Went a wee soul, straight and clean,
Who clasped, as Christmas bells rang clear …
The tiniest evergreen.

I Saw the Child King

I saw the Child King that first Christmastide
And knelt in silent prayer at his side,
For I was then, but who, I do not know.
But this I know, I gazed upon his face.
There was a golden light, a mellow glow
That entered in the room and drowned the place.
It was not candlelight, nor from the skies,
But the light of love, which shone from Mary's eyes.

I may have been a shepherd, for they say
That shepherds heard the voices as they lay.
They heard sweet angel voices in their sleep,
And rising up, they saw the shining star,
And bowing down in worship left their sheep,
And guided by the heavens traveled far
To the Christ Child in His lowly resting place,
To gaze upon the glory of His face.

I may have been a Wise Man come to sing
My worship and my praises of my king ...
Come with my gifts to kneel beside Him there ...
My gifts of gold and frankincense and myrrh ...
All in the noble garments Wise Men wear,
To call him King, and Mother-Queen for her.
I may have been a Wise Man from afar,
Who came in faith and following a star.

They say a shepherd, answering the call,
Took up the smallest lambkin of them all,
Too small to leave in desert night alone,
And carried it to where the Christ Child lay.
Perhaps that lambkin, by the manger throne
Knew his Lord on that momentous day ...
Perhaps it was in that way I did share
In that great night, and silent, worship there.

I may have been the keeper of the gate
Who, knowing the decree, did hesitate
To let them in, but seeing close of day
Approach, did give them leave to go
Where the stables were to rest upon the hay.
And later, seeing bright a golden glow
Upon the stable walls, did go to see ...
Then knelt me down to worship ... silently.

I saw the Christ Child that first Christmastide
And knelt in silent prayer at his side.
For I was then, but who I do not know,
But this I know. I gazed upon his face.
There was a golden light, a mellow glow
That entered in the room and drowned the place.
I saw the Child King that first Christmastide
And knelt in silent prayer at His side.

———

The Empty Stocking

What shall we put on the Christmas tree for him?
His stocking slim
Hangs on the mantel there,
One of a pair
He'd hardly worn at all.
They'd be too small this year, and he
Could almost reach the star upon the tree.

I wonder if he sees the star somewhere
And reaches out his hand to touch it there ...
Or if the evening sky his vision bars
With a Heaven full of bigger, brighter stars.
What shall we put on the Christmas tree for him?
His stocking slim
Is such an empty one.

My son, my son ... if I could make you live,
My life I'd give, my song to you,
That you might singing go that whole life through.
We'll sit and think of you this Christmas Eve.
This is our gift. We shall no longer grieve,
But we will think of you, my son, today ...
The gift God gave and had to take away.

The New Year

I am youth.
I have been wondering about the new year,
And now I know its purpose.
It is for me.

It is a period of time set aside,
Created, dedicated to me, to my dreams.
There are tall, silver towers I shall build,
And words that I shall speak will change
The course of nations.

I am the serious youth,
The laughing youth,
The scholar, the athlete,
The child of America,
And this new year is for me.
I am age.

Another new year. I am glad to see it come.
I shall be glad to see it go.
I'm just a little tired, and I found that there's
No such thing as time.
Time is but the period between birth and death.
No more.

I am age, the wise old age …
Experienced age …
The strength of a nation,
And conqueror of time.

**** Written at the age of 17****

New Years – 1937

I feel a kinship with those minute green
Leaves and plants that waken in the Spring.
I ... I who felt so old at seventeen,
All just because I hear a few bells ring

And see tomorrows stand in long, straight rows.
I who never thought beyond today ...
All time and life unfolding like a rose
With petals new to sunlight's shining ray.

I hear soft laughter faintly through time's veil,
And sorrow sobbing somewhere in the year.
At seventeen, a heartbreak isn't new,
And everyone must sometimes shed a tear,

And this year's love ... yes ... I must change that, too.
For somewhere ... somehow ... it has lost its sheen.
I wonder that I ever thought it true,
For loves are light when one is seventeen.

Somewhere, not long ago, I lost the past ...
Today, last night, and all my yesterdays.
I was so sure some cherished things would last,
But I have learned that nothing ever stays.

I often wish that time would have me stay
Like plants in spring ... and little childish things,
But gazing on the stair-steps of the day,
I know the urge to wake and try my wings.

The House That Jack Built

Jack built a house,
A house on a hill,
A funny little house
For Jill.
There was love at the windows,
And love at the door,
There was love in the shadows
That fell across the floor.
There was love in the sunbeams
That touched the roof with gilt,
The funny little roof on the house on the hill,
The funny little house that Jack built.

Jack showed the house,
The house on the hill,
The funny little house
To Jill.
But Jill wanted mansions
Great, and of stone.
Now Jill has a mansion.
She lives all alone.
There aren't any sunbeams
To touch her roof with gilt,
And she weeps for the house, the house on the hill,
The funny little house that Jack built.

There's no love at my windows,
No love at my door.
There's no love in the shadows
That fall across the floor.
There aren't any sunbeams to touch my roof with gilt,
And I weep for the house, the house on the hill ...
The funny little house that Jack built.

Wanted: A House

Wanted: a house, the right size for two.
It must have a porch, and a room with a view.
It must have a window where rainbows are spun,
And where the canary can sing in the sun.

Wanted: a house where dreams can begin,
With nooks and with corners to keep the dreams in,
So, there will be room for the tables and chairs
And all of the things a well-dressed house wears.

Wanted: a house. A pink one would do ...
A little pink house with gay shutters of blue.
No matter. We'll paint it with sun-paint at dawn,
Spill color all over the sky and the lawn.

Wanted: a house that hides by a hill,
With pots of geraniums set on the sill,
Where the moon comes to visit in evening gloam
Down a pathway of silver. Wanted: a home.

Through the Gap in the Hedge

I am a builder of hedges.

That is why
When I had found the house I had dreamed ...
A house with little blue doors
And windows that looked out to flowers and sky,
Windows that listened all the day to the singing of the birds
And the whispering of the wind,
I said, "This is my corner of Heaven ...
A Heaven with little blue doors."

That is why
I built my hedges high.
And now I have learned
There can be no hedges 'round Heaven ...
That blue doors must stand open,
And windows can grow blind.
There was a gap in my hedgerow.

That is why
That I remembered long-lost laughter
Learned from a little gray house,
A house with a chimney that pointed nowhere,
And a porch that creaked and vanished in flowers and grasses ...
Framed in the gap in my hedgerow.
And I thought, "There is something there holy,
And so, I must widen the gap."

Why did I
Build my hedges so high?
Yes. Now I have learned.
Now the hedges lie low, and Heaven
Comes to the house I had dreamed
Without stepping over.

I was a builder of hedges.

That is why
I almost lost dreams and nearly laughter,
From my house with the little blue doors.
But now I am teaching my lilac to bloom,
And the birds to sing, and the winds to whisper again ...
And teaching my windows to see.
I've opened my little blue doors to the sky
Where broken hedges die.

———

Blue Door to Nowhere

My dancing feet have reached their gay path's end
At this blue door, set in a vine-clad wall,
A wall that bounds the real world's edge but for
A door that leads to nowhere and to all.

And I, a child of summer sun, whose kiss
Is warm against my mouth, shall not lament,
But thankful I shall be for even this,
These glimpses with which I must be content.

For I have seen beyond the blue door when
The twilight has come down across the skies,
Beyond it in a woman's tired face,
Beyond it in a baby's sleepy eyes.

And I shall fashion keys of urgent laughter,
And mimic birds, and mock the fairies' call
'Til someday I shall open for you, after,
Blue doors that lead to nowhere and to all.

———

NONSENSE

Aola, mother of six, 1960

The Sneep

Beware the snithering little sneep.
Avoid his habitat,
Because the habit that he has
Depends on where he's at.

He dearly loves to daily tread
The warm, cerulean waters
And raise his little pointed head
To snoggle at your daughters.

He doth avoid the early morn,
But 'neath the tropic moons
Will flower forth with wit and corn
And checkered pantaloons.

He'd rather far be dead than wed,
Sleeps only when he's sleepy.
Though sneeps aren't men, it's often said
That men are very sneepy.

Death of an India Rubber Man

He tied himself into a knot
And in that knot he stayed.
A Boy Scout couldn't tell just what
Kind of a knot he made.

So, pretzel shaped, he grew quite thin.
He lost weight by the ounce.
He lost his vigor and his vim.
He lost his snap and bounce.

He tried to scratch his shoulder blade
But soon grew short of breath.
His ribs were all that he could reach.
It tickled him to death.

The undertaker did his best.
His coffin was quite round.
They crossed his ankles on his chest
And rolled him underground.

My Heart Lies in the Sun

In dawn of time, when time began,
A thing came from the sea
To find on earth what thing it was
And what it wished to be.

It crept across the barren coast
And through the dripping wood,
And in the desert found the sun
And found that it was good.

So, in the desert, on a stone,
My heart lies in the sun,
And just a shell walks in the town
In masquerade, alone.

Temptation

The wind came in the window
And sang a song to me
Of love and buried treasure
And lands across the sea.

I laughed at wind, I laughed at love
And bade them go away,
For my bread was in the oven
And the children were at play.

The wind blew out the window,
And soon the happy bunch
Of children all came trooping in
For kisses and for lunch.

***** Aola Seery, published at age 17,
Golden Harvest, Mistletoe Press, 1937*****

A Writer's Chains

Link
Upon link
The writer strains
To forge himself
A set of chains.

And fastened to it is the weight
Of knowing he's inadequate,
Yet, as he drags his clanking fetter,
He smugly knows his chain is better.

Unclaimed Treasure

The fairer flowers fade the first
For they're a rarer breed.
So, isn't it nonsensical
That men who're common-sensical
Pass up the bloomin' weed?

Turn About

I put a chain around her neck …
That stuck-up, prim Miss Jones,
And fed her prunes and broccoli
And threw out all the bones.

I put flea powder in her hair
Though she hadn't any fleas.
"Now wasn't that a splendid dream?"
Asked the little Pekinese.

"It was that," said a poodle
Of a very brilliant nature.
"I think that we should mention
To the Lap Dog Legislature,

"Or at least the Canine Congress
A game of turn-about,
And try these dames with feather brains
And take and turn 'em out."

"And then what?" asked the Chinese chow
When he had got the floor.
"Well," said the petted poodle,
"We could turn about some more.

"Now, broccoli is not half bad …
Nor even spinach greens."
"Ten days on turnips," said Pekinese,
"For communistic dreams."

Genius

If I chose to run about in furs,
And wear not sock nor shoe,
Folks would say, "How very shocking!
What's this old world coming to!"

If I were, oh, so famous,
They'd care not how I went.
They'd say, "See children … Genius …
That's why she's different!"

The ladies all would copycat
The things that I would do.
But since I am not famous,
They'd say, "She's lost a screw."

And since I'm not a genius,
Nor a lovely movie queen,
I cannot run 'round barefoot,
Nor paint my toenails green.

The Trillipede

A-slooming in my slumpsy chair
And sipping burpsy mead,
I thought I saw, beside me there
A purple trillipede.

Whence comest thou, oh Urply Worm?
I say, what brings you here?
He ooched a little closer then,
And snubbered in my beer.

"I say," I gurped and guffed a bit,
"You wish a friendly chat?
Leave us discuss the Demican
And the Republicrat!"

'Twas then I felt a chinkling chill.
His eyeballs pinkly rolled.
My backbone thistled in my chair.
The room grew churkly cold.

Then blithered in a bitsy thought
Like lightning snackling by,
To wit, 'twas either him or me,
Or rather, he or I.

I quickly flumped him in my glass,
A "trillipede eraser,"
I sang and drank him down. Alas,
I found there was no chaser,

To chain the gobbering guest I drank,
Subdue that snurkling cup.
He'd won his weevily way, hands down,
Though he was bottoms up!

Quadropotamus

And there's the quadropotamus.
It never has such troubles.
Since "quad" means four, it swims ashore
And pairs off in mixed doubles.

Fantasy

My mother was a wee mouse, playing in the heather.
My father was a bullfrog, croaking out the weather.
My birthplace was a black tarn, high up in the hills,
And I drink up the Dewy cup of yellow daffodils.

All night I dwell in fantasy
Until the world is waking.
Then it's hie away, my fairy fey,
The cold grey dawn is breaking.

In deepest shade by fern fronds made,
I laugh with sides sore aching
At the silly greed and the useless speed,
The foolish world is making.

*****Aola Seery, published at age 17,
Golden Harvest, Mistletoe Press, 1937*****

Intentions

He planned to build a patio
With pros and cons and yes and no.
He wrote down figures and dimensions.
He had such serious intentions.
Then he found how many bricks it
Would require and didn't fix it.

The Unicarp

The unicarp's a lonely one,
Or fish, or bird, or bug,
For "uni" means there's only one,
No mate to snerk and snug.

So, when life seems to piflicate,
Your weegil starts to warp,
Be thankful you can goggernate!
You're not a unicarp.

Trisexoderm

Pity the trisexoderm.
No mating is allowed.
One-third of it is always firm
In stating, "Three's a crowd."

If two are he's and one's a she,
You'll hear a he declare
That Poker is the only game
Where three will beat a pair.

A full house never does occur.
The species is exterm …
Oh, how much better off you were
Than the trisexoderm.

Would-be Sinner

I have made my crown of thorns,
And each thorn is a sin
Which did not reach fulfillment,
But's just a might-have-been.

****Written at the age of 18****

They Say

They say that I am fatalistic,
Cynical and Pessimistic,
And they are just as right as rain,
But should you, Love, come back again,
I'd lose my lessons in Life's school,
And be an optimistic fool.

Short Short Story

Mother says, "I hate a kitten!"
Daddy says, "I hate a cat!
You may never have another one,
And that, my child, is that!"

They were, oh, so very angry
When I got a cat to keep,
But I heard them playing with it
When they thought I was asleep.

TV

Before the living room TV
My lovely children lie,
And stepping o'er their prostrate forms
To reach the kitchen I

Do wonder at maternal love
That in misguided bliss
Doth make them swallow vitamins
And lets them swallow this!

If This Be Your Idea

If this be your idea of love, then take it!
For after all, it does take two to make it!
If I must kneel to you, and worship so,
And garner but the few crumbs that you throw,
Then take elsewhere your poor pathetic feeling
And search out one who's more adept at kneeling!

Mother's Prayer

Four small faces soft in sleep,
Lashes curve on downy cheek,
Hair like fans of brown and gold,
And I, heart full of love to hold,

Remember sharp words said today,
And choose this quiet time to pray.
God, let me from this full store borrow
Strength and patience for tomorrow.

To Hear You

Time and again my trust I give.
Time and again I rue it.
You tell me what you will not do,
And then you go and do it.

You say my wish is your command
And that you will obey it.
My every whim you understand
And that I'm but to say it.

Your love's so very big, my dear,
You cannot say nor spell it.
You never loved another one.
That is, to hear you tell it.

Housework

Housework in the kitchen …
I don't want to do it,
Though I have a feeling
Later on I'll rue it …

Rather write the rhythms　　The day my house is shining
Forming in my head.　　　　Like any housewife's pride,
The day I do not hear them,　Put on a band of mourning.
That's the day I'm dead.　　That's the day I died.

Problem in Higher Mathematics

If my heart were an apple that could be
So easily broken in two,
Then I could give, you plainly see,
One half to him, one half to you.

But my heart's not an apple that could be
So easily broken in two,
Yet how can I give it all to him?
How can I give it all to you?

What Shadows Do

The night was light with moon, and oh, so sweet,
And as I watched, I saw our shadows meet
Upon the grass, and gently kiss each other.
I thought awhile perhaps I should tell Mother,
But I am not a tattletale, 'tis true,
And Mother doesn't care what shadows do!

Waterlogged

When I long to see the mountains high
I find a book to read.
When I wish for a wave's caress,
A hot bath fills the need.

And since I cannot see the world,
Must live with dreams befogged,
You'll have to take me as I am,
Well read and waterlogged.

****Dedicated to "Me" - 1960's****

Claustrophobia

Within a room
Within a house
Beneath a sky,
Boxed in a box
Within a box
Am I.

Trapped in a trap
Within a trap
We folk
Could prove to be
God's biggest
Gift-wrapped joke.

Joe Bill Garrett

In Granddad's time
A place was set
For Joe Bill Garrett.
It is yet.

The lamp that sputtered
With wind about,
The candles guttered,
Have all gone out.

At family tables
Family law
Provides for a man
We never saw.

Plastic and silver
For pewter and tin.
A guest who's a ghost,
Not kith nor kin.

In Granddad's time,
A place was set
For Joe Bill Garrett.
It is yet.

Pals

We stroll by the sea,
My friend and I,
With the wind in our faces,
Clouds sailing the sky.

We sit on the sand,
And I make remarks
At the sun on the sea,
But my friend only barks.

He's a cranky old sea-dog.
Looks mean, and he growls,
But he's humorous sometimes.
Why sometimes he howls!

You'd like to meet him?
Why surely, why not?
Shake hands, Cap'n Barlow,
With my best pal, Spot.

***** Aola Seery, published at age 17,
Golden Harvest, Mistletoe Press, 1937*****

Mother - Poet

There's a couplet in the morning
On newborn, shaking legs.
I am in the kitchen
Making scrambled eggs.

There's a sonnet in the nooning,
A queen with golden crown.
No time now for mooning.
Biscuits turning brown.

There's a triolet in evening ...
Bouquet of pain and peace.
I sift the flour and brown it
In bubbling bacon grease.

Where have all my poems gone?
Eaten, every one.
Nibble
Nibble
Nibble ...
Like a cinnamon bun.

To an Erring Relative

All talked about and frowned upon and quite unhid
Are all the things you should not do ... and did,
And from my moral pedestal, it's good to know
The things I longed to do, and didn't, do not show.

Awkward Angel

A halo I had, and the winsomest wings,
But I knocked them all off on the edges of things ...

The edges of anger, the edges of hate ...
Persuasion, evasion was always too late.

I stayed far away from the center of sin
But the edges of love singed my wings to the skin.

I'll never be lonely, this I can foretell,
On the edges of Heav'n or the edges of Hell.

The Cabbage and the Rose

A little green cabbage in the garden grew.
Its cabbage head was aching, and it felt very blue,
For a red rambler rose had just cut it dead
And called it a foolish little cabbage head.

So, the days went on and the rose looked down
On the little green cabbage in its leafy gown,
'Til one day the gardener, as still as a mouse,
Took the rose and the cabbage into the house.

He put the red rose in a crystal vase
And placed it all on a cloth of lace.
"Aha," said the rose, "at last I see
They're all going to kneel and worship me!"

But alas, when the cabbage came through the door,
There was room on the table for nothing more,
But the Master wrinkled an ecstatic nose,
"Put it in the center there. Remove the rose."

My Sins and I

I took my little secret sins
Down to the creek to drown,
Five cunning ones of black and white
And two of shining brown.

I set them down in one long row
And bade them meditate
Upon their foolish wicked ways
That led them to this fate.

They looked at me so wistfully
And promised to be good.
I yielded to their pleading eyes
And hid them in the wood.

But when I had reached home again,
There, perched upon my sill,
Were all those naughty sins of mine!
And they are with me still!

Comparison

A merry-go-round
Is a musical powder box grown up.
A water well
Is an oversized edition of a cup.

A true friend's heart, could we but see,
Is 1000 times the whole,
For such a heart must surely be
Of a size to match the soul.

*****Aola Seery, published at age 17,
Golden Harvest, Mistletoe Press, 1937*****

Secrets

I told secrets to a daisy
With eyes of purest gold.
Someone told my secrets.
I guess the Daisy told.

My friends told all my secrets.
I dare not scold them lest
I lose their precious friendship.
"They meant it for the best."

I told secrets to my fireplace.
The hazy wood smoke curled
Up the crooked chimney -
Spread secrets to the world.

It does seem rather tragic,
When of friends I have such wealth,
That I should get so lonely
Telling secrets to myself.

*****Aola Seery, published at age 17,
Golden Harvest, Mistletoe Press, 1937*****

I

I'm afraid that I have an impossible complex.
I'm one of those people, a doer or die.
I get some strange notion that stirs my emotion,
Irrepressible, unguessable I.

I often have longings, these turning-out-wrongings,
Though Mother and others cry stop,
And I just can't resist, though they make me desist,
Making snoots at a traffic cop.

I make holes in hedges, I walk on the edges
Of cliffs. I'm a doer or die.
So, watch lest I trip you or a garter snake slip you,
Irrepressible, unguessable I!

Revenge

Impish little shadow!
Watch it run and caper!
Tangles words up in my brain
That won't go down on paper.

Just wait! I'll catch it napping!
What will I do to it?
I'll wait until it quiets down,
And then I'll walk right through it!

Survival

So much attention now is paid
To muscle form, to wit
The world is based upon, it's said,
Survival of the fit.

And at the table they're repaid
At each required repast
With accolade and marmalade ...
Survival of the fast.

Our striving siblings, strong and pure,
Of whom we're very proud,
Go one step further to insure
Survival of the loud.

And we'll be lucky when they're wed
If each young heir apparent
In social columns to be read
Lists one surviving parent.

Conformity

Were I like you
And you like me,
And all the time
We'd just agree,

And had no woe
Or poverty,
No barriers
Of space or sea,

And had like numbers,
Or like name,
And each of us
Saw God the same,

I think 'twould be
An awful shame
For each to be
Another's double,

Since God has gone to
So much trouble.

TIMES AND PLACES

Oklahoma country girl, Aola – 1935

Last Night

It was such a lovely night,
Warm and faint and dim.
The moon was just a shaft of light,
Strange and curved and slim.

Jasmine blooming at night's feet
Sent fragrance to the skies.
Night pressed her soft, warm woman's hand
Against my weary eyes.

The night was warm and faint and dim,
The moon a shaft of light.
Nothing happened ... no stars fell ...
'Twas just an April night.

Wings

Wings in the night
When winds grow chill,
And the geese are flying high.
Wings in the night across the moon,
Against the autumn sky.

Wings in the night,
They blot the stars
And suddenly are gone.
Sometimes I think they are lost souls
That just keep flying on.

*****Aola Seery, published at age 17,
Golden Harvest, Mistletoe Press, 1937*****

I Remember a Time

I remember a time … it was long ago,
At least a hundred years or so …

The sight of the sun and sound of a dove,
Arms full of roses, heart full of love.

The roses have wilted. The time is long since
And that is the only difference.

Heritage

When the god Thor walked the mountains,
And Neptune strode the seas,
Apollo sent his sunbeams down
On the wings of Balder's bees.

Now in the veins of modern man
Flows blood of gods and kings.
The sun which shown on Ulysses
Now glints on Lindberg's wings.

***** Aola Seery, published at age 17,
Golden Harvest, Mistletoe Press, 1937*****

Laughter

Today is such a happy day!
I couldn't wish for more.
When I awoke this morning
I found outside my door
Laughter
After
This long night,
Beneath the pale moon's beams.
She has been smoothing pillows
And giving children dreams.

Spring

He who lives each passing day
And loves each rising sun,
Who sees his neighbor's feet of clay,
Yet loves them, every one,
Who sees his faith renewed, fulfilled
As Aprils come and go,
Is first to see the lilies bloom,
And robins in the snow.

Anew In Springtime

Begin anew in springtime.
That was what they said.
So, I must find a new love
For the old one which is dead.
But can a new love flower
Where late has been but pain,
Or live a single hour
Where tears fall bitter rain?

But I shall seek out springtime,
And nothing shall I say,
But, oh, in folding little dreams
And putting them away ...

Memories

Brave and bright in rows they stand.
How strange, I had forgot
That somewhere I had seen before
Zenias by a cottage door,
Geraniums in a pot.

Once I felt the sifted dust
Sun-warmed on thorn-scratched feet
And sought verbinias by the road
And rode the hay-racks fragrant load
Through the sleepy waves of heat.

But why must I remember?
Think thoughts that give me pain?
The smell of hay from fragrant mows,
At dusk the coming of the cows,
Fresh fields, new bathed in rain?

*****Aola Seery, published at age 17,
Golden Harvest, Mistletoe Press, 1937*****

You, Oklahoma

You, Oklahoma, with the soft winds blowing,
You, Oklahoma of the deep blue skies
And heart-breaking sunsets in the west glowing,
Oh, the sight, the delight of you to my eyes.

There is such a thing here as true dreaming
In the hills and the skies and the waving grain,
The mellow dreams that to be are seeming,
Where gladness and sadness have been … and pain.

Here power is. There are great things growing,
And here there is magic and a mystery
In red earth with a black gold flowing
From its crimson wounds in an ebon sea.

Oh, Oklahoma of the granite boulders
With food for a world in your golden bowl,
With a mantle of cotton on red shoulders,
In you are power and a dream and a soul.

It's all mixed up with a soft wind blowing,
A heart-breaking sunset, a sky that is blue,
Gold waving grain and black gold flowing,
The self and the soul and the heart of you.

Royalty

Gay is the life ahead of me
And richness it doth hold,
For I am born to royalty,
The purple and the gold.

Gold Oklahoma sunsets,
The hazy purple plain,
And purple shadows in the depths
Of waving golden grain.

My land has golden pumpkins
And blowing goldenrod,
For what more could a person wish?
--This country and a God.

I hope that I may come to lie
When all my race is run
Where plains stretch purple to the sky
And fields shine in the sun.

*****Aola Seery, published at age 17,
Golden Harvest, Mistletoe Press, 1937*****

Flying South

The gray goose flies south
Where blue skies smile.
I would follow after,
But I'll bide a while.

The gray goose flies south,
Shadow in the sky,
So like its call is
My soul's lone cry.

The gray goose flies south,
My soul takes wing,
'Til the gray goose flies north
Come another spring.

Leaves

There's a heap of magic
In a heap of autumn leaves,
And my heart is fast entangled
In the witchery it weaves.

A little breeze once told me
The bright leaves charmed the snow,
And soon there'll be a snowflake
For every leaf I blow.

And there will be a snowman
For every bare brown tree
And sleighs and sleds and jingle bells
And childish shouts of glee.

Oh, there's a heap of magic
In a heap of autumn leaves,
And my heart is fast entangled
In the witchery it weaves

*****Aola Seery, published at age 17,
Golden Harvest, Mistletoe Press, 1937*****

Eternal Change

I thought all things were hard and cruel
-- Was about to give up trying.
Then I heard the wind cry 'cause the leaves
All in the fall were dying.

I said no one had pity left.
No sooner was it said,
Then snow clouds swept o'er fallen leaves
And covered up their dead.

I even doubted happiness
'Til a bird began to sing.
My blues blew away with winter.
One can't be sad in spring.

*****Aola Seery, published at age 17,
Golden Harvest, Mistletoe Press, 1937*****

Prairie Pictures of Autumn

Autumn invades the valleys
And smiles through lavender haze
While jack-oaks on a hillside
Smolder into a blaze.

Corn shocks rise like Indian teepees
Under skies of flawless blue.
Day is soaked in mellow sunshine.
Night spreads her curtains, stars shine through.

Maples flame in dying glory,
Scattering leaves like squandered gold.
Quails call out from hidden corners.
Chattering jays in chorus scold.

Goldenrods and yellow sunflowers
Curtsey in the sumacs red,
And in orange and crimson riot,
Orchid carpets now are spread.

Drowsy murmurs of contentment
Offer hymns of praises sung,
While a partridge in the coppice
Signals to her straying young.

Freeway

When this bright ribbon was laid down
From our town to your town,
The wheels turned and wheels are speed.
But underneath, the earth's dark need
Thrust forth, and failing, kept its seed
For wheels must turn and wheels are speed.

Suns rise and set, and days all pass,
And man is as the leaves of grass,
And wheels are speed, and wheels must turn.
Who feels the seedling souls that yearn
To know the sun, to live, to learn?
Yes, wheels are speed, and wheels must turn.

And he who thinks
And he who feels
Must stop the wheels,
The turning wheels,
Must pause and think
Among the turning wheels.

New Fields

For this land of tawny waters
We chose crimson and the silver,
Chose as patterns our forefathers,
Free men, brave men, pioneers,

Men who built their land unaided.
We shall work and build as they did.
Build a beauty and tradition
That will linger through the years.

Where the red buds fire the hillside
We shall dedicate to honor
All our lives and pull together
That our standards high may wave.

There are new fields for the taking,
And new trails for the making,
For we are the builders of today,
The pioneers, the brave.

*****Written by Aola Seery at 17, Northeast High School, Oklahoma City, Oklahoma, Golden Harvest, Mistletoe Press, 1937*****

You, I Love

If I can write a word and you can see
The washday of a North Dakota sky,
The clean and stringent smell of laundered clouds
Strung out from lake to land and hung to dry,

If I can write a word and you can hear
The susurrus of silk in Kansas corn,
The whispered step of mist in gray ballet
Along marsh grasses in the early morn,

If I can write a word and you can feel
The thunder's power, the trembling of a dove,
This, then, is the world and all to me
For if I reach you, you I love … oh, you I love.

I Am the Very Only Fairy

I am the very only fairy
Who stays awake in January.
I live in dead and blackened stumps
Or grass in small frostbitten clumps.

The world is old I look upon,
For summer's come ... and summer's gone,
Yet this month which I have chosen
That I might melt tears that are frozen

And touch the cold, wan moon above
With fire to warm the heart of love.
These, and a small child's merry laughter
Repay for summer's sleeping after

When, far from summer's sun and rain,
I sleep, night-blind, to tears or pain ...
I am the very only fairy
Who stays awake in January.

———

Northland

The witching moon, her wanness spread
About the massive mountain's head,
Outlining branches bleak and dead
    Against the snow.

Bends blank white face on blanker space,
Where soft and slow men hold no place,
And wolves win oftener in the chase,
    In the chill moon's glow.

*****Aola Seery, published at age 17,
Golden Harvest, Mistletoe Press, 1937*****

La Selva Encantada

In the enchanted forest, La Selva Encantada,
Stands pine and quaking aspens,
The birch and bending grasses,
While sonorous and mournful
Rolls the organ of the forest.
And the birch bends to the mountains,
And the aspens quake and quiver,
For Pan lives on the mountains
And he thunders hymns to Heaven,
Wild and weird and somber
Like the birches and the aspens
From the enchanted forest.
La Selva Encantada.

*****Aola Seery, published at age 17,
Golden Harvest, Mistletoe Press, 1937*****

April

April is a weeping maiden,
But though she smiles through dewy eyes,
Her tears are really tears of laughter.
Her hands are full of glad surprise.

Mirror of Life

Reflections in a pool.
A silent, bleak-far-down-ness to a tree.
And here Death lies in stilly depths. Let be
This living world, and come and gaze with me,
Far down.

Reflections in a pool
A strange and chill tranquility is this,
A darkness here and Death's cold deadly kiss.
I wonder, hence, upgazing, shall I miss
This place?

Jeweled Hill

A half-frozen bee in a field of dead clover,
A lone gray goose goes flying over,

The wind shrills … stills … in a fit of sorrow,
The leaves all sigh, thinking of the morrow,

The night slips by on its velvet feet,
Leaving a broad snow-crystal street

For the cold gray world to walk upon
As it rises to face a cold gray dawn,

'Til the sun steps out in the morning chill
And tints a snow-capped, jeweled hill.

March

March is a time for mending things
Like fences, and feathering friendship's wings

With a friendly smile and a deed or two
To help someone that you meant to do

Just yesterday, or a month ago.
March is a time to get to know

Your neighbor, and get to know his need
And help him and profit by the deed.

Spring doesn't come with the bloom or the swallow.
Warm your heart and another's, and spring will follow.

In the Hollows

Frost lay heavy in the hollows
'Neath a sky of cloudless blue,
Where the Morn had draped her mantle,
Ghostly web of frozen dew.

Mass of color, mass of shadow,
Stood the trees between the hills,
Twisted jack-oaks, tinted beauty,
Ice caps crowning laughing rills.

Then Morning gathered all the leaves
And left, for Morn must go,
And Darkness walked on snowshoes through
Trees stark against the snow.

*****Written at the age of 17*****

Sunset

The frosty, vermillion sun
Gets out of bed at early dawn
And jumps and comes on the run
And throws yellow rays o'er the lawn

And tosses beams 'cross forests green
And throws light on decks of ships at sea
And on the farmer's corn and beans.
He never lingers ... no ... not he,

But goes on and on and on
Across the great, wide world,
Nor partial is he to rich or poor
'Til he reaches world's end
And goes to bed, his red rays furled.

Home Work

I love the canning time at home
I really, truly love it,
The hustling and the bustling,
The heat and flurry of it.

No time to sit and scribble
Or lie around and dream
When you're canning in the kitchen,
And the kitchen's full of steam.

I guess that I'd give up my dreams
Of fairies and of elves
To help with canning time at home,
See jars on cellar shelves.

*****Aola Seery, published at age 17,
Golden Harvest, Mistletoe Press, 1937*****

Moon Tears

I wander steeped in misery
Beneath the moon in Tripoli.
Why must that mad moon follow me
When my heart's whole is over sea
         And in another land?

I've gone from homeland hills and dales
Through weird uncharted ocean trails,
But still above my head it pales
And tints with silver dust the sails
         And shines upon my hand.

A moonstone on my finger glows
And with the moonlight brighter grows,
A simmering symbol of my woes,
A moon tear fallen to repose
         In shining silver band.

My moonstone told me tales of old,
Of fame and fortune bright it told,
Of Irish eyes and pirates bold,
So, I went in search of fame and gold
         Far from my native land.

Oh, Moon, thou hast thy watch to keep …
Thy glittering crop of stars to reap.
What wouldst thou have? Why dost thou weep?
A cake to bake? A floor to sweep?
         Instead of waved-washed sand?

Oh Moon, weep not in discontent,
For thus I wept, and thus I went,
From home and love and country rent,
My fame forgot and fortune spent.
                In discontent I stand.

I'll fling my moonstone over side,
And flinging it lose pain and pride,
Set sail and from the harbor glide
Before the changing of the tide,
                Back to my native land.

Oh, Moon, when I'm far oversea
Don't weep for me. Don't weep for me,
    Forever lost to Tripoli
And gold and fame and mystery
              Found in the foreign sand.

Come visit me when I'm at home
Far from the calling surf and foam.
Shine thru the trees in evening gloam
    In dappled pattern on the loam
              Far from the ocean sand.

At midnight, when the world's asleep,
I'll call, "Oh, Moon, no longer weep.
I've a cake to bake, a floor to sweep.
Thou hast thy glittering stars to reap
                Here in my native land.

***** Aola Seery, published at age 17,
Golden Harvest, Mistletoe Press, 1937*****

When Today is Yesterday

I built a tower stone by stone
Until it pierced the sky
And let the little sunbeams out
Around my tower to fly

And burnish it, and polish it
And keep it shining gay,
Keep it bright and shining
When today is yesterday.

I sent for very finest stone,
A very special grade of
Eternity and true strength mixed
With the stuff that dreams are made of.

I dreamed of it, and builded it.
I built it strong to stay.
It will be there, standing still
When today is yesterday.

***** Aola Seery, published at age 17,
Golden Harvest, Mistletoe Press, 1937*****

One Brief Hour of April

April flings her banner of azure o'er earth
At the turning of April, the sound of her mirth.
Then it's over the hill with me, over the hill,
Where the days with their sun-gold the deep hollows fill.

It's over the hill and down to the sea,
Where winds are a whisper and scented with tea,
And cedar and teak and sandalwood, too.
Where dark eyes are dancing, and bleak eyes of blue

Scan seas to the east, and seas to the west
Where white-winged ships cling to the sea mother's breast,
Scan seas to the north and seas to the south,
Where ships cut the foam to the harbors far mouth.

Oh, I'll watch the sea and the ships coming in
And wonder at each and at where it has been ...
Then it's over the hill again, over the hill,
While April still lingers, and blue skies are still,

'Til I come to the edge of a dear little town
Where fragrant white blossoms are still drifting down
Like tiny white ships, and they'll say unto me,
"Home is the sailor, home from the sea ..."

And all the while April will glow with her mirth,
While spring flings her banner of azure o'er earth.

―――――

Mushroom Towns

Before this land was old to man, nor less than almost new,
Upon the prairies broad expanse, the mushroom cities grew.
Across the plains, from hill to hill, the long, red furrows ran,
And wild things wheeled and sped in flight from this, the hand of man.

Smoke rose from cabin chimneys or perhaps a trading store
To lie along the hills where smoke had never lain before.
They built their cities in a day beside the crystal streams,
Just as we built our first ideas, our ideals and our dreams,

Foretellings of the wealth and power to someday be instilled,
The first faint touch of dreams and such to someday be fulfilled,
But thus were cities dreamt and built and thus the cities grew,
Before this land was old to man, nor less than almost new.

Progress

It's to be torn down. Yes, that cabin there.
There they're going to build a mansion of the modern mode.
The roof is sagging with its weight of years,
And the heavy timbers creak and groan beneath their heavy load.

It's to be torn down. The ancient oak beside it bows its head
　　Remembering when the cabin was alive and gay
　　With happy children, memories long since dead,
　　　　Memories of a bygone day.

It's to be torn down. Progress is always cruel
　　For the new the old makes way,
　　And on forever this way it will go
　　While men on earth hold sway.

*****Written in 1930 at the age of 10;
Aola Seery, published at age 17,
Golden Harvest, Mistletoe Press, 1937*****

The Wanderer Returns

I have never seen the harbor half so beautiful as now,
　　But perhaps my heart has never been so still.
I have seen the ships sun-tinted, but a moonlight gilded prow
　　Holds a tranquil peace for one of rover's will.

I have never seen the harbor half so beautiful ... patched sails,
　　And swaying, swinging lights against the gloam ...
Canvas beaten, buffeted, and blown by foreign gales
　　Resting in tranquility at home.

I have seen the world in glory and a sunrise on a hill
　　And sun-paint on a pirate's black-flagged prow.
But I believe that never has my wild heart been so still
　　Nor the harbor half so beautiful as now!

First Snow

Autumn lost her golden sandals here
And, running barefoot through a chill night's hush,
Ran headlong into Winter's silver spear,
And died there where that ghostly sheeted bush
Burns bright with crimson berries in the wood …
Burns bright with crimson berries … or with blood.

Now, this morning as the valley wakes,
Slightly shivering, half numb with the cold,
A murmur runs along the glassy lakes,
As in the dawn their drifted banks unfold,
Where once the shores ran down to blue with green,
Is white, with purple shadows in between.

Here the willow to the frozen ground
Bends long, brown fingers searching in the snow,
Where Autumn might have walked. A crystal mound
Has covered all her footprints long ago.
This bush with its crown of dying embers …
All of Autumn this white world remembers.

Salute

Once I saw a gallant ship
'Gainst blended sky and sea
And smiled to see her colors dip
In fealty to me.

Her anchor lay in new washed sands,
Her tall mast pierced a star
As she lay in harbor to await
The crossing of the bar.

I'd like to be a gallant ship
With a gay flag in my hair
And a cargo full of friendliness
And lots of love to share.

Then, when came time I should depart,
I'd dip my flag to thee,
And disappear as good ships must
Where the sky blends with the sea.

*****Aola Seery, published at age 17,
Golden Harvest, Mistletoe Press, 1937*****

The Entrance to Fairy Land

There is a hill … a strange, dark hill …
That bars the entrance to Fairy Land,
And on soft, dark nights, when the wind grows still,
And Pan's pipe calls like the whip-poor-will,
My soul and I go hand in hand

Where shadows lie in a soft, dim cloud
Of darkness deep and darkness still,
And the whole world sleeps in its fragrant shroud,
While the hours stand still and the trees stand bowed,
Through the entrance to Fairy Land.

Peaceful Hollow

Here once there stood a quiet church, unpainted, small and gray.
Here great trees grew and towered tall and made a shadowed way.
Here quiet people, sober dressed to Sunday worship came,
And the small gray church at eve was lit by true faith's shining flame.

Here now the evening sky is pierced by church's towering spires,
By glowing light and candle lit … but where are true faith's fires?
I stood and mused upon this thing and heard the organ play,
And wondered if strength, years, and growth made one forget to pray.

An Interview with Dame Nature

"I'm from the Daily News," I said.
"I've come to find out all
About your famous recipe.
What's your recipe for fall?"

"Curling smoke and autumn leaves,
A jack-o-lantern's grin,
Then always (this is not required),
I put some mischief in.

"Then Turkey legs and tummy aches
And wild geese flying high
And goldenrod high on a hill
Against an autumn sky.

"A heaping cup of thankfulness,
A pinch of chilly weather,
Take apples, pears and pumpkin pies
And mix them all together.

"Now, Miss, you have my recipe
Go on! Now get out! Shoo!
Go away! My land, a body'd think
I had no work to do!"

**** Aola Seery, published at age 17,
Golden Harvest, Mistletoe Press, 1937*****

Prairies

Fifty years ago this land, the land we love was young,
Its red plains still untouched by plow ... its praises still unsung.
But stretching far, from sky to sky, unclaimed, and still untilled
Were prairies hiding molten gold, rich plains on which to build,
And purple shadowed prairie wheat, unbought, and still unsold,
Stood fragrant in the gentle breeze and rooted deep in gold.

As pioneers came here in search of land with richness filled,
So did we seek a higher plane on which our lives to build.
They found a wealth of purple plains that stretched from sky to sky.
We found the prairie lands of life that on these plains do lie,
Just as the pioneer who came to seek the sun's last glow
As it sank on western prairie land of fifty years ago.

Fairy Music

Shrills a strain
Of moody elfin music, piped to greet
Soft slanting shadows striving to awake
The slim dim moon, cloud mantled in the lake,
Fluted fairy music, faint and sweet,
Muted music, mad and strangely sweet.

Sweet the song,
A lilting mad, yet melancholy plaint,
'Til dawn, when back to crystal caves they creep,
And dew-wine drugged, they sing until they sleep
Fluted fairy music, far and faint,
Muted music, far and sadly faint.

**** Aola Seery, published at age 17,
Golden Harvest, Mistletoe Press, 1937****

April Fool

I remember, I remember what my grandma used to say,
"He who's a fool in April is as big a fool in May."

And then she added, chuckling, as she heard a wedding tune,
"There's fully twice as many fools … we all are fools in June.

"July and August, choose a man, and follow right behind him,
And should you seek a fool, by chance, it won't take long to find him.

"And in September," so she said, "seek not a fool at noon.
Glance anywhere down Lover's Lane, beneath the harvest moon.

"October finds them everywhere … in city, country, schools …
A killing frost was never known to trouble any fools.

"Since fools, like all things, grow with age, they're bigger in November
But the biggest fool of all, you'll find, is somewhere in December."

I remember, I remember what my grandma used to say …
"He who's a fool in April, is as big a fool in May."

Thank You Note

Thank you for your Christmas gift.
I loved it more than I can say …
Perhaps because it was from you,
Perhaps because, on Christmas Day,
Those who love should be as near
As we two, and as dear.

Thank you for your Christmas gift.　　Thank you for your Christmas gift.
It meant so much to me.　　　　　　　It tells a tale to me
Perhaps because I shan't grow up …　Of love, and care, and tenderness
I'm still a child, you see.　　　　　　And Christmas days to be.
And I shall treasure, dear, always
This day, this Christmas Day.

Two Songs

Much of the tawny water of Oklahoma has flowed down to the sea
Since you came, Oh, Red Bud,
And many moons have poured their light into the hollow cup of the earth,
Glowing on the beaten copper of the waters,
And glinting on the copper-penny profiles
Of Oklahoma's people.
Aye, many moons and many suns have shown,
Slanting down in waves of warmth and light
To find and greet your welcome feet, Oh, Red Bud,
And the waters which flowed in sunlight to the sea,
And all the moons which shone, and all the blazing suns
Have told me of you, and they sang two songs,

And they are these.

Oh, Red Bud, you are Woman,
Scarlet lipped and lissome,
Crimson lipped and smiling,
And curving to the sun.
Inscrutable and haunting,
Mysterious, and leaning
In the brilliance of your beauty
Where the red, red waters run.

Oh, Red Bud, you are Woman,
Slim in blinding beauty,
Standing on the hillsides,
Sighing on the plain,
Lovely, yea, and luring,
And the world comes at your calling,
And you hold men's hearts and dye them
With your red mouth's scarlet stain.

Oh, Red Bud, you are Hunger,
Stalking barren prairies,
Shadow-gaunt and bitter
In the huddle of thy hate,
Clinging to a hillside,
Naked fingers bleeding,
Grim against the hillside
Like the shadow hand of Fate.

Oh, Red Bud, you are Hunger,
Skulking in the dimness,
Secretless in sunlight,
And robed in Hell's own flame.
Hunger, yea, but luring,
And the world comes at your calling,
And you hold men's hearts and dye them
In your life-blood's scarlet stain.

Much of the tawny water of Oklahoma has flowed down to the sea
    Since you came, Oh, Red Bud.
And many moons have poured their light into the cup of the earth,
    Glinting on the beaten copper of the waters, and
    Glowing on the copper-penny profiles of Oklahoma's people.
    Though many moons and many suns have shone,
    Never has their light found fitter mate
    For this, their well beloved land, Oh, Red Bud.
    All the waters which flowed in sunlight to the sea,
    And the moons which shone, and all the blazing suns
    Have told me of you, saying, "Sing these songs."

    And I have sung.

*****This poem was awarded second place in
the Red Bud Contest, Poetry Society, 1939*****

Old Trails

There's that about old trails at eventide
That takes one's breath away, pervades one's mind.
For along these starlit trails is written clear
The happiness and hardship of mankind.
For they who trod these paths knew naught of ease,
Yet found within the beauty of the plains,
And in these ghosts, these silver-dripping trees,
A recompence and solace for their pains.

There's that about old trails at eventide,
Old trails thru fields of waving, golden grain,
Of battle 'gainst the warring elements …
The wind and sun, the snows that heaped the plain.
Sad is the tale, yet somehow it is sweet.
I feel it all as haunted trails I ride.
I feel it all and pause with bated breath …
There's that about old trails at eventide.

****Aola Seery, published at age 17,
Golden Harvest, Mistletoe Press, 1937****

LOSS AND SORROW

Aola and Bill
Awaiting Separation by WW II
San Antonio, TX - 1943

A Dark Moon, Always

I shall tremble when I see
A dark moon, always,
And know remembered ecstasy
Down night's dim hallways,
Ghost-flowers in a scented night,
Hush'ed winds and fairy flight,
And taste again the cup of tears
From pale, dead hands of memory
Across the barrier of years.
I shall remember ecstasy
Where perfumes lie, a fragrant cloud
On this dead garden of my dreams,
Dim in its shadow-woven shroud.
I shall remember ecstasy
In brushing wings in fairy flight,
And I shall tremble when I see
A dark moon, always.

The Door to My Heart

For long and weary years I cried
For him I'd learned to know too late,
Regretting, too, I'd played with fate.
When Life's autumn skies turned gray,
When grief seemed all that came my way,
By chance I saw sweet Love come near.
My heart cried out, "Oh, enter here!"
But Love replied, "I cannot stay,
For I, myself, have learned to play!"
Now … maybe 'twas chance …
I fear it was Fate,
And the door to my heart
Was opened too late.

Coffined

Coffined so early and coffined so surely,
You live in a frozen town.
Do you ever long for a gypsy song
Or wish for a velvet gown,
Or a world that is upside down?

Long are the highways but stronger the by-ways
And bare are the dust-brown feet
With the red-heeled shoes for the rendezvous
In the hedgerows where two paths meet
Where the berries are twice as sweet.

We follow the piper to fields that are riper
And dance to the Pipes of Pan ...
You've sold your soul for a sieve full of soil
And a seat on the stage of man
And ended before you began.

But you still long for a gypsy song
And wish for a velvet gown ...
Coffined so early and coffined so surely,
You live in a frozen town.

Tonight

The arms of Winter hold me close and chill,
  Shrill weeping for my love song lullaby.
When did I hear a summer night wind still,
  Or Love breathe out its beauty in a sigh?

The arms of Winter hold me chill and pale,
  There was a sweeter song, sung ever low,
As carved seraphs tremble at Wind's wail,
  And yet there was a Summer ... years ago.

And Summer's dusky hands held close the fire,
  That flamed in tender night, in mystery.
The breeze drew muted murmurs from its lyre,
  And eve was drowned in depths of ecstasy.

Summer, fleeting, left the arms of Night,
And Beauty put the flame out with her tears ...
How strange that I should think of you tonight,
  For it has been so many, many years.

I Wish I Knew

Why should I weep?	Why should I shed
Why should I cry?	So many tears?
With silent tread	Minutes ... days ...
The days pass by.	Weeks and years.
Why should I weep	Why should I weep
For things untrue?	For only you?
I wish I knew!	I wish I knew!

Ghost-Love

Oh, many ghosts of little things,
The little ghosts I cannot name,
The flickering of ashy wings
Above the candle flame ...

How many times I've drowsed to start
At some forgotten dreamt-up face.
A languid hand has touched my heart
And left a frozen place ...

And while I've trembled at a touch,
And feared the small things night winds move,
I wonder why I feel so much
To dream of an old, tear-drowned love.

Of marbled halls I sometime walked
There is no stone to touch and feel.
There are no tones of tongues I've talked.
How can this ghost-love seem so real!

Portrait from a Castle Wall

With tranquil face and still, quiescent hands,
I gaze at you from out an old gilt frame.
I am as old as this ancestral hall.
Perhaps you do not even know my name.
But this you think as you stand watching there ...
Oh, she was beautiful, and she was fair!

She must have known the quietness and peace
That grows from out of calm serenity.
She must have never hated, never loved,
To have been pictured thus ... tranquility.
All this you think while gazing on my face.
She belongs in this old hall ... this quiet place.

Fool! Can't you see the soundless things that rise
And pace the hall with silent, measured tread,
And can't you hear the voiceless anguished cries
That echo from these walls, nor see the dead
That rise to take their places once again,
And dry tears strive to wash away a stain?

A slender hand ... a pale, quiescent hand
Once held a sword, a bloody, dripping sword.
A tranquil face can hide a secret well.
Peace? Peace, you say? No, that is not the word,
For, painted here in velvets and in lace,
My eyes are secret in my tranquil face.

Yesterday

Oh, we were happy in our play,
    We and the wind together.
We told sweet lies, and from the skies
    There fell a raven's feather,

And then we played awhile at truth,
    And, oh, the truth was bitter.
We wept to find the wind grow chill
    And see our flowers wither.

We saw our worlds turn into dust,
    Our sunshine into rain,
And found sweet lies would not bring back
    Our happiness again.

I cannot see tomorrow,
    But I know it can't be gay.
How could we be so happy,
    So happy,
    Yesterday?

Winter

A worshipper of sun I am, and still
    Apollo hides behind a southern hill,
And drawn before me chill and dark and gray,
    A blind across the window of his day

Excludes my soul. So, cold I walk, alone,
A pagan one whose God has turned his face.
    I carry in my breast a frozen stone.
    Hell is a very cold and lonely place.

A Chilling Rain

'Twas on a rainy afternoon
      When Spring was in the air.
I let the rain make diamonds
      Of spring-song in your hair.

And then a summer afternoon
      So sudden was the weather,
I let the rain fall in between
      And we were not together.

And so, in Winter's stormy pain,
      I feel rain's frozen dart,
And though I let it take my love
      It shall not break my heart.

Why Do I Sigh?

Why do I sigh?
The music that the piper plays is sweet,
So sweet I put my silver sandals on,
And, dancing, lost myself in tangled paths.

I had not cared
For singing any song was ever sung,
Or dancing to a dream, a singing dream
That any slant-eyed piper chanced to play.

But I have come,
And here there is a doorway in a stone,
And here the piper enters with his song.
There is a cloud half-drawn across the sun.

The door will close,
And I shall beat on stone with bleeding hands
And listen for a music that is lost.
The music that the piper plays is sweet …

The music that the piper plays is sweet …
Why do I sigh?

Why Do I Weep?

Why do I weep? Because my days are bright days,
And I shall never want for anything.
Why do I sigh? Because my ways are light ways,
And all my winters will be touched with spring.

I shall remember chill and bleak Novembers
We knew together. Now that we're apart,
I shall long for that time always and remember …
No April ever warm my bitter heart.

Seeking an Ember

Seeking an ember bright, you came
Riding across a moat of flame
Calling my name.
And the pity of it I should see
Only your tranquility,
And praying that the fires should cease,
Reached out for peace.

Seeking an ember bright, and yet
I knew not what you came to get.
Now, to forget
Is as impossible a thing
As to hold back the tides of spring.
And you, oh, you could never know
Peace I needed so.

Oh, strange it is that fire is chill,
And peace can sear a windswept hill;
That fire should long for peace, and yet
Peace searches, embers bright to get,
Finding, when the day has died,
Fire and frost unsatisfied.

———

Bitter Autumn

I thought if I climbed an autumn hill
And stood so still, and stood so still,
With autumn leaves twined in my hair,
Perhaps some God would see me there,
And thinking I should be a tree,
Make me one and leave me be.

The pain you brought, I would forget,
But still I feel … remember yet.
My branches sigh with mournful sound.
My golden leaves are drifting down.
Brave and chill I stand apart,
The symbol of a bitter heart.

Chilly Winds

Somewhere I have seen soft days
With gently feathered hedges,
Soft warm days with soft warm ways
Somewhere beyond the edges

Of this harsh world of chilling winds,
Of brittle frozen grasses,
Too cold to catch a fleeting ray …
Reflect it as it passes.

Sometimes I think the keening wind
Has frozen stars to stones
And blown them from forbidding skies,
And I walk on their bones.

Mourning

Days tumbled over each other
In haste to hurry by ...
Now march in a slow procession ...
Swell of a mourner's sigh.

If I had only known more soon
That ceasing of your song
Would make those days that seemed so short,
Grow lonely, and so long.

There Is No Place

The world's so wondrous and so wide
That it reduces me
In stature and astounds my eye
With its infinity.

Yet in its vast and shadowed ways
That one could hide and die in,
In all its tangled thoroughfares,
There is no place to cry in.

The world's so lovely and so long
It runs from pole to pole,
And still, it shelters little things,
The swift hare and the mole,

But strange it is the echoing
Of shattered hearts ne'er ceases.
In all this world there is no place
To sweep the broken pieces.

Forgotten Youth

Our sons went to the battlefield,
That man-made hell of hate
Where death held court and death had sport,
And darkly hovered Fate.

The whole world came to help us weep,
And sighed to hear us sigh.
Remember though your hurt was deep,
'Twas the bravest way to die.

I saw another group of sons
All lying still and white,
Additions to the highway's toll.
The headlights were too bright.

The whole world came to help us weep,
And sighed to hear a sigh.
The world can't salve a wound so deep.
They were too young to die.

The world forgot it all too soon, | The world forgot times gone before,
And just the other night, | Forgot our hurt and pain.
I saw another group of youths, | Fate hovered darkly in the skies,
All lying still and white. | And death held court again.

**** *Aola Seery, published at age 17,*
Golden Harvest, Mistletoe Press, 1937****

Discontent

I lay on a stone in a dusk-darkened stream
With the day and my gaiety gone,
And a wan silver disc had slipped out of the wind
To turn all the star candles on.

Aye, turn all the candles on, Wan Moon,
That the night might never die.
Let me lie steeped in sorrow and full of woe
For there is no one so woeful as I.

The stream, leaping silver with light of the moon
Claimed my fancy, but bitter I cried.
"You are but reflection! Yes, you and the moon!
Reflecting the light that has died."

Aye, turn all the star candles on, Wan Moon,
And light up the world for me.
Faith and fancy have flown and this stone where I lie
Is as hard as reality.

Too long have I hungered and reached for reflection.
The light that's so lovely too often is chill.
The moon is a ghost, and the stars are wax tapers
That twinkle and glimmer and never are still.

Aye, turn all the star candles on, Wan Moon.
With this cynical world, I'm forspent.
What havoc was wrought where they shook from the tree
The apple of discontent.

***** Aola Seery, published at age 17,
Golden Harvest, Mistletoe Press, 1937*****

Footsteps

Soft are the footsteps of a dream.
No footprint does it leave,
No sight or sound that it has been,
No reason to believe ...

Yet I have wakened in the night
Between the dark and dawn
With trace of tears or secret smile,
A lost dream wholly gone.

A Stranger to These Ways

I have gone down again into the town.
I traveled light the weary miles, and lone,
But, oh, the changes in the town since yesteryear …
I turned me home.

I have gone down again into the town.
I stand and gaze about the village green.
In the hustle and the hurry of the crowd,
I've lost my dream.

I dreamed I should go down into the town
And stay there, when I went to town again,
But the sturdy, honest village folk I find
No longer plain.

And now that I've come down to town again,
I am a stranger to these streets and ways I see.
How strange was my belief that naught would change
Excepting me.

When Fashion, Fuss, and Feathers come to town,
Simplicity and Commonplace will leave.
I should be glad for progress come at last,
But yet I grieve.

I shan't come down into the town again.
A many weary miles it is, and lone.
I shall retrace the weary paths of yesteryear,
And turn me home.

Filing

If I am sighing in the night,
If I am crying in the night,
Time is flying ... in his flight
Are things I have not done.

But I keep smiling in the day,
Whiling half my hours at play,
And filing all my nights away,
Forgetting every one.

A Moment There

A moment there, I thought I saw a ghost,
But now I know it was not, could not be,
For ghosts must once have known a spark of life.
Reality.

And now I know this foolish dream of ours,
For dream it was, that I have treasured most,
Has never flamed to being, chilled in death.
A moment there, I thought I saw a ghost.

Forgive me, then, the moment that I dared
To think we had again a dream to share.
It was only that I thought I saw a ghost.
A moment there.

Never Cry

When your heart is heavy, dear,
And all is done, or said,
Never, never cry, dear.
      Laugh a lot instead.

When your dead heart's wrapped, dear,
In lavender, and lace,
Greet the gray old world, dear,
      With a smiling face.

That is what they told me,
But, oh, the pain is such!
I never knew not weeping
      Could hurt so very much.

Two-Ways-Going

Fairy lanterns sway on slender stems
Where shadows slant from hush'ed trees and dream
To the music of the singing water reeds
Which Pan tunes to the cadence of the stream.

Somewhere, sometime, I know I lay, a shadow,
And learned the songs that soft gray twilights bring,
And this is why our paths are two-ways-going.
Somehow, I learned no song that two could sing.

Perfection

My dear, this wood of holly, smooth and white,
Is like your soul, so languid, free from stain.
This placid piece does not cry out in pain,
Or in its grain show ought of sweet delight.
Like a Madonna's hooded eyes, the sight
Invites no sweet departure from the sane
And sets no fire to dream within the brain,
To smolder and to seethe, to blaze up bright.

So, I shall bow the knee, my dear, to you,
And standing far away from you admire,
Which is the thing that you would have me do.
Oh, build your dam of dreams against desire!
Then, having worshipped at your shrine, I, too,
Shall take myself away in search of fire.

Spinster

I stood so long to think upon the world,
The world which lay outside my garden gate,
That ivy vines grew strong and held it fast.
It ever was my way to hesitate.

And when the elfin Springtime showed me how
To break my fences down and heed her call,
I closed my eyes and told my eager heart …
You have seen Springtime's jewels die and fall.

And now I sing my song of outer worlds.
My empty voice falls on an empty room.
The flowers I plant inside my garden gate
Take root and thrive and never, never bloom.

Today

I shall not weep until tomorrow,
Though the skies are leaden, gray.
If the sun should shine tomorrow,
I shall weep my heart away.

In the long line of tomorrows,
I'll recall today's great sorrows,
But I'll be smiling, brave and gay,
Today.

Last Night I Dreamed

Last night I dreamed I saw two mockingbirds,
And then but one was left, for one was flown.
And, oh, my heart was breaking for the bird
That sang alone.

Last night I dreamed I saw a high stone wall
That wore a single rose, and my heart broke,
So sad was I when someone plucked the rose
And I awoke.

Last night I dreamed, and yet, somehow today,
On looking in your eyes, I want to weep.
Today I watch you grow away. Tonight,
I shall not sleep.

A Man Wants a Son

Ol' Maria sits in the sun, grim and gaunt,
A-tended by the gal thet she didn't want.

'Tis a lone lorn land fer a gal, God knows,
Less'n she's worn to the ways and woes,
To the molten metal of sun that spills
On a stretch of sand between hot hills …
And a man wants a son, a son the worst.
It wasn't good thet a gal be first.

Ol' Maria sits in the sun, grim and gaunt,
A-tended by the gal thet she didn't want.

These are hills of hunger, and plains of pain,
With a thirst fer tears as well as rain,
'Taters in the straw stack, corn out yonder,
Li'l gold prairie flowers plowed in under …
Glad when the boy come! A man wants a son.
A gal can't git the plowin' done.

Ol' Maria sets in the sun, grim and gaunt,
A-tended by the gal thet she didn't want.

And there by her side, her granyoung'ns play,
Pushin', shovin', gittin' in the way …
An' not far away, in a cottonwood,
'S a thievin' boy in a hangin' hood.
And people don't care, as they ride on past,
Thet a gal was first. Thet the gal is last.

Ol' Maria grieves in the sun where it's hot,
A-tended by the only child thet she's got.

The Fisher's Wife

Down the path, on black nights when the sea
Was reaching up for ships to deck its floor,
She came, and held her lamp that he might see
And set his sails again to rocky shore.

Down the path on black nights, twenty years,
When waves flung mighty walls against the gale,
She held a lamp for weary eyes to see.
For twenty years she waited for a sail.

And no one told the tale of driftwood found
Where waves had folded in against the sand,
And no one spoke a ship's name that the sea
Ironically had given back to land.

But no one was surprised when last she cried,
"A sail! A sail! God has been good to me!"
And holding close her dead lamp to her side,
Stepped out ... and out ... into the swirling sea.

———————

Scottish Ballad

A gentle eve was damped wi' tears,
    As tenderly they kiss't,
And opalescent clouds grew dim
    And turned to amethyst.

Oh, I s'all miss ye, Laddie,
    But ye must gang awa',
Your duty to the King's mair great
    Than luve a'twixt us twa.

So, here's a rose, fo' luve, Lad,
    A lily, wet wi' tears,
And a bonnie bit o' heather
    T'light the lonely years.

Oh, he held close the red rose …
    Would hold the heather yet,
But Death placed in his cold hand
    The lily, wi' tears wet.

And, oh, she greets, and doesna spin,
    And at each sound does start,
A puir, pale wistfu' little ghaist
    Gangs wandrin' through her heart

An' sings the saddest little song
    About when luvers kiss't,
And opalescent clouds grew dim
    And turned to amethyst.

Might Have Been

I have spent my days in weaving
    From the sun unto the sun,
Lovely little patterns of
The things we might have done …

Lovely little patterns of
The might-have-been-shared years.
I hid them from the sunlight
And laid the dust with tears.

But now, tonight, I have come back
    To things as they now seem.
I've snapped the thread of mem'ry
    I raveled from a dream.

I've been too busy brewing
    My sorrow in each tear …
Now my idle heart must break
    With loneliness, my dear!

Divorce - An Abstract Impression

I wander alone. Alone. Alone.
The sky is pale, and the air is thin,
And the snickering sound of the frozen grass,
Sere and crisp in its cage of glass,
Is the only sound of the world I'm in.

I wander alone ... and cold. Alone.
There is no song in the ice-bound stream,
And the chill holds my mouth in a frozen smile.
It may be a step, or a frozen mile
To the embers left of some warm old dream.

I wander and seek and find a stone.
But I cannot rest ... I must seek a flame,
And the sound of the stream is a wintry moon.
How cold it is, how old I've grown,
And there is no warmth in a spoken name.

How cold it is, and how old I've grown,
As I wander alone. Alone.

Why Have You Come to Awaken Me?

I have dreamt the years away,
Wrapped in shadows of my own weaving,
Pain-dulled poniards of my own grieving,
Guarding against the day ...

Why have you come to awaken me?
Safe-hid from a hundred morns,
Long in a world of shadows lying,
Brier-walled from the world of crying,
With sharp pain-poignant thorns.

Sun surges in like a golden sea.
Why have you come to awaken me?

Growing Blind

So long ago, in springtime's wind
I saw with childhood's eyes, unblind,
People were not merely faces,
Places were not merely places,

But colors and the edge of sound
Were feeling, painful as a wound.
And joys were reds
And sorrows blues.

Tears tear the heart,
And laughters bruise.
There is no sun to light a day
When people and a place are gray.

I close my eyes in summer's sun,
Becoming blind as anyone.
He, who will not hurt too much
Must close his eyes and never touch.

Now

Now I can say your name and toss my head,
For fires that were have long since ceased to smolder,
And I can meet the world without a dread,
Shrugging pity from imperious shoulder.

And I have even met you face to face
And smiled and spoken as a stranger speaking,
And there has not been a recurring pain,
None of my heart's mad voiceless anguished shrieking.

Yes, I have met you, and the world, and day,
And even joined in our remembered laughters ...
If I could only sweep the cobwebbed stars
Of worn old dreams that cling to night's blue rafters ...

Quest

I wonder why it is that we
Have not what we desire,
That Jane may long for dancing shoes,
And Fayre a cozy fire
And socks to mend and babes to tend,
While Jane longs for the lights
And muted music throbbing through
The sultry tropic nights.

Yes, Jane will sit and dream her dreams
Of far exotic places
And overlook the loveliness,
In laughing, childish faces,

And Fayre will dance in silver shoes
Far, or far too small,
And dream her dreams, her futile dreams
That won't come true at all.

I wonder why it is that we
Have not what we desire.
Jane longs in vain for dancing shoes,
And Fayre a cozy fire.

I wonder why it is that all
Our dreaming is in vain ...
That I should weep for Fayre, my dear,
And you should weep for Jane.

I Shall Write Again

When I go to my own small house
And close again the door
And touch the fire upon the hearth,
Then I shall write once more.

When I shall feel against my heart
All of each stranger's pain,
And match his sorrow with my tears,
Then I shall write again.

When I can close my door at last
Against a storm-wild night
And hear the voices in the blast,
Then once more I shall write.

But since the elemental things
Are closed against my ken,
I shall not mock my silent muse.
I shall not touch my pen.

Retribution

Across the world and o'er the world
      And through the world went I,
And I saw some stars in a blue, blue bowl,
      And I stole them from the sky.

And then, to hide their silver eyes
      Which were so bright, so bright,
I placed them 'neath a velvet cloak
      I stole away from night.

Now, home again at Robber's Cave,
      I find the cloak is pain,
And the stars I stole are silver tears.
      I shall not steal again.

Unstrung

I can remember once upon a night,
A shallow cup of velvet filled with light,
Looking at the sky and wondering whether
There were some way stars could be strung together.

They were like that to me, the starry string
Of hours we spent so long ago in spring,
A scattering of stars to light me nightly,
Unstrung, and with no clasp to hold them tightly.

Pray, Be Kinder

If I should in a sudden moment cry
The name that is forever on my heart,
If I should in unguarded instance sigh,
Or cease to hide the swift sad tears that start,
Then, pray, be kinder than you ever were,
And leave me, that I may this pain endure.

If I should chance to see in you again
The things I knew. If you should turn and smile,
To thrust me with that stabbing sword of pain
That wounds me, slays me every little while,
I pray you, go away, and leave me be.
There is no blade so keen as sympathy.

How can I live when my heart doesn't beat?
How can I die when you still hold me here?
To see your face afar, to sometimes meet,
Is but to fall upon a poignant spear,
And yet there is no death that peace can give.
I must live to forget … forget to live.

The Precipice of Silence

The precipice of silence … oh, how often, hand in hand
We tried to scale its stony steeps that someday we might stand
In silhouette against the clouds, against that azure sky,
That dumbness of our tongues be loosed, that our love we might cry
To all the world, cry each to each, but like an upflung sword
The precipice of silence stood between us and a word.

The precipice of silence ... we climbed up it half the way.
Then you were gone I know not where, and I was left to stay.
Halfway we gained, and then you tired, and weary, tempest-blown,
You found a greater silence than the one that we had known,
And standing there so lonely, I heard ringing in my head,
The echoing of little things, the words we might have said.

The precipice of silence, and I've gained the top alone,
And looking down the path I came, with briers overgrown,
And tangled into thorn trees across the beaten track,
There is no way again to you. There is no going back.
Poor dead unspoken little words lie limp among the years.
The pathway down the other side leads to a sea of tears.

I Must Remember

There is an answer to everything,
To life and death and breath,
And the darkness of hills against the evening sky. But I
Have heard the echoes laughing at nothing,
Laughing, pealing, and whispering across the empty canyon,
Seen hill-stones tossed into the valley lands by unseen hands,
And dark trees praying to a stormy sky,
And that is why
I must remember the answers to everything.

There is an answer to everything.
To sun and rain and pain,
And the depth of secret darkness in your eyes,
Like skies before a storm.
Cloud-laden.
Warning.
But there will be no rainbow in the morning.
There is naught but muted thunder in your eyes.
A bridge of lies
I watch you building, heedless of Truth's cry.
And that is why
I must remember the answers to everything.

———————

Buried Treasure

I found a Locket that I hid
So very long ago
When the whole world wept with roses
That had not known the snow.

A spider's web was woven,
All woven round about,
As if to seal its secrets in
And seal the whole world out

I placed it in the shadows,
Back in its shadowed place.
It does not need be opened.
I'm haunted by that face.

I placed it in the shadows …
This bit of age-dulled gold …
Such things are best unopened,
Some stories left untold.

*****Aola Seery, published at age 17,
Golden Harvest, Mistletoe Press, 1937*****

I Shall Not Miss You

I went to Death, but Death was not for me.
I could not still the beating of my heart.
I heard my heart's sound drumming in my ears
Like the stumbling march of many futile feet
Toward the finite grave. Hearts do not still
At will.

I went to Life, who flung her scarlet robes
Aside and clutched her gray shawl close against the chill.
I saw no joy in her bleak eyes, nor tears,
But just the blank monotony of time.
No laughter in her kingdom did I see
For me.

But I shall find some little thing to do.
I let my garden grow to thistles while
I tended other gardens. I must staunch
Thorn wounded roses bleeding on the wall.
I shall not miss them as they die and fall ...
At all.

Transformation

We stood before you. One and one, with love for you, were we.
I was a Lord o' high estate. A Gypsy lad was he.
The world went 'round and mattered not, for we were three - were three.
You had a loving smile for him, and but a tear for me.

The Gypsy lad has proven him a lord in all these years,
And I have gone to Gypsying and conquered little fears.
The Gypsy lad has won a name, and I, applause and cheers.
He proved him worthy of your smiles, I ... worthy of your tears.

A Woman Scorned

I could have taught you dreaming,
Shown the way to rainbow's end.
You chose instead the sophistries of life,
To look away from high hills and from sky,
And follow beaten paths away from me.

I could have taught you dreaming,
For I have seen, when midnight turned too swift,
The startled look of Pan within your eyes.
Life is a futile thing when Pans cease dreaming
Or seek out glories other than the dawn.

Because of this, a shaken earth shall quake,
And you shall wake to thunder in the night;
See lightning blaze and flame in flashing light,
And see strange shadows lengthen in the lake.

Because of this, the sea shall rise and break
Against cold stone in all its bitter might,
And sea gulls stir their wings in sudden flight,
And tongues of sticks and stones and such awake.

For all my tears, my poor weak bitter tears
Cannot put out the fires that rise and hiss
Without your warming arms and tender kiss
Against the long futility of years.

You will awake to thunders in the night,
And you will see the lightning flame across the sky,
Remembering I could have taught you dreaming.
So shall the lightning lash the helpless meres.

To sticks and stones I give my name to cry,
And they will speak with tongues that shatter dawn,
And when the fog comes groping from the sea,
And you are lost from dawns, do not forget,
I could have taught you dreaming, shown the way.

Half-A-Child

Your teasing smile inspired in me a wild
And elfish laughter, and your tenderness
A wild desire, an impulse to caress
Your tumbled hair. You called me half-a-child,
And I was happy then, because you smiled,
And did not check my swift impulsiveness,
Nor ever dream that you might love me less.

Now there is no returning. I beguiled
You for a single hour, and suddenly
You thought you found a deeper, lovely dream,
That quiet grace could love more tenderly,
And I have aged with tears that start and gleam,
And for what all my new maturity,
The quiet pool that drowned a laughing stream!

Sometimes

Sometimes in the dusk when there is no wind
And the evening comes in a voiceless tide
And heartbeats are thunder, muffled and tied,
Then the savage turns to his savage kind,
Song in his soul, murder in his mind,
Straining at the steel with his savage pride,
Straining at the bars that are strong and wide,
And peace and plenty are the bonds that bind.

For the old, dead days, they are not dead dreams,
And they cry their life in the pagan rhymes,
And they weave their ways into new world schemes
With the same dead deeds and the same old crimes,
And the old cries form in their voiceless screams
When there is no wind in the dusk sometimes.

Katie of the Salt Marsh

Katie in the salt marsh, the little winds are crying
Because they can't remember the banner of your hair.
The winds in the salt marsh are keening and they're sighing
In a last vain hope that they'll find you there.

Katie in the salt marsh, the grasses there are bitter
And frosted with the spray from the gray face of the sea,
And the white, sick moon that is hung there in the winter
    Walks in the salt grass a-searching for thee.

Oh, Katie of the salt marsh … and Katie, oh my bride,
The small winds miss you sadly, the grass is touched with blight,
    Oh, and can't they see you here, a-walking by my side?
    Why must they wake me from my dreams tonight?

    The dream of us walking as we did so long ago,
Walking there and talking there of dreams we dreamt would be.
You, with your silken hair and the way that it would blow,
    In a great salt wind with spray from the sea.

    But, oh Katie of the wind, and Katie of the rain,
    My Katie of the salt marsh, my Katie gone away,
The wind is in the grasses and the sea moans with pain …
    Wakes me from my dream and my dream won't stay.

    The wind from off the salt marsh is cold in September…
    While lonely here the grasses sway, I walk up and down …
The old ones shook their heads and said … well I remember …
    Flowers from the salt marsh can't grow in the town.

———

Selling Memories

He sold them all ... or gave them, some folks said ...
The wooden rocker and the featherbed,
The bureau made of wood and nailed with wood ...
It was so old, and no one understood
He thought that he was selling memories.
He thought that he was selling smiles and tears.
He thought to close a book of reveries
By selling fifty years ... long fifty years.

He sold them all ... her cherished, priceless treasures
Culled from years of weeping and of pleasures,
Boxed, and sight unseen, her treasures sold,
And with them dreams more precious far than gold ...
The crazy quilts ... and then the afghan throw ...
The thimble, and the small, gold-handled shears ...
He sold the thought of how she'd sit and sew,
By selling fifty years ... long fifty years.

He said, "I'll go ... perhaps a change of scene ..."
But he will learn he cannot kill a dream,
And he will come back to this place again,
And he will learn man cannot turn back time
To days of dawning youth and fairer skies ...
And then one day he'll know that she is near,
When a welcome sunset blinds his weary eyes.

Someone Should Have Told You

Not long ago, my dear ... and my surprise
Is that no one has told you, long ere this ...
Before you thought to kneel, before to kiss
  A silent creature with death in her eyes,
I died. Oh, no, I pray you, do not rise.
And do not take what I must say amiss.
Death is a chasm dark, a deep abyss ...
That self may cross alone as the soul dies.

And when you cannot hear your own heart's beat ...
  And there is not another dream to know ...
  And there is no more cold, nor is there heat ...
  And hot tears burn your eyes but will not flow ...
  And nothing in the world is ever sweet ...
Oh, someone should have told you ... long ago.

Waiting

I waited at the gate a lonely hour,
And tried to send my thought to meet your thought.
But somehow, in the gentle night, 'twas caught
In webs of fragrance from the perfumed bower.
A shadow fell across my cheek ... a shower
Of shadow rain by moon and willow wrought,
And through its gold-laced lattice, I was taught
Enchantment of perfection from each flower.

And standing there, half leaning on the gate,
Sunset and moonrise more than I could bear,
Without one thought of you, or cursing fate,
I saw eternity while I was there.
And that is why I come again to wait,
Why, when you do not come, I do not care.

The Second Prayer

There is no deed not lost once in the trying,
And no dream lives that has not known one dying.
God sometimes waits to hear the second prayer ...
So, since my life is tangled in your hair,
And in your sweet grave eyes, my dear, be knowing
That where you go, there I, too, shall be going.

And though with futile tears my eyes should glisten,
I'll say my prayer as long as God will listen ...
There is no deed not lost once in the trying,
And no dream lives that has not known one dying.

You Will Not Know

The reason that I love you, I suppose,
Is that I know you well, so very well,
The look that all your face wears in repose,
The thoughts you think, the things you start to tell.

And I have seen your thoughts, and one by one
Have counted each and put it in its place,
But when a small child's bright hair caught the sun,
I saw the gentleness that touched your face.

And I have seen you weave a rainbow bright
With just a smile to banish every gloom.
My silver mist of tears has vanished quite
To see you lift your eyes across a room.

You pause to say goodbye. The open door
Looks out upon the world, and we must part.
You do not, will not, know that you were more
Than passer-by ... a stranger to my heart.

Somehow I Do Remember

Somehow I do remember you a wall,
A wall that I might cling to as a vine
Sends out its reaching fingertips to twine
About the heart of stone. I do recall
Sometimes you smiled. Not too much. You were tall.
But those were not the things that made you mine.
You were the bread I sought, sick with the wine
And wonder of the world ... sick with it all.
Now, though I have found others twice as kind,
And only felt an echoing of pain,
The haven of a wall I cannot find,
And now I know there'll never be again
The hearts of stone and roses intertwined
Against the driving slant of wind and rain.

Mist Against the Window

It is not strange that I should think of you
When autumn skies dawn crisp and blue,
When the whole world has a song ... a song to sing,
And one could not be sad for anything.
I open wide my windows then, and I
Can see your face against the autumn sky.

But why I think of you, I cannot say,
When leaden skies dawn chill ... dawn chill and gray,
When, mist against the window, rain appears
Like someone's tears ... the sky's slow steady tears.
I see your face in everything, and all ...
Against the sky ... the hills ... my dark blind wall.

I, Who Remember

Leaves quiver golden, and I, who remember
From somewhere and sometime an October lane,
Shall go again seeking that somewhere and sometime,
To live in that somewhere, that sometime again.

Leaves will fall withered, and you who've forgotten
The somewhere and sometime, will once more forget,
But I shall be waiting there ... I, who remember,
I, who remember, remembering yet.

When leaves are all fallen, then I, who remember,
Shall go again, slow again, when skies above
Are angry and gray and the wind whispers sadly,
To heap my dead leaves on the grave of our love.

It Will Not Seem Strange

I recall how you wept when I gave you the roses.
You named me a dreamer. The memory clings,
For you wanted bread, and a roof against rain,
And the sight, the delight of substantial things.

I recall how you wept when I gave you the roses.
You wanted a haven, the strength of a wall
And wool of the warmest to weave for a jacket.
I gave you a rose and a gay Spanish shawl.

I recall how you wept when I gave you the roses.
It will still not seem strange when one of these morns
You'll come to me asking a rose that is withered,
The love that I gave you ... and heedless of thorns.

The Disillusioned

I started on the high road,
Well equipped for life,
But the things the maiden carried
Were too great for mother, wife.
One by one the extras I discarded in defense,
And I left my sensitivity
hanging on a fence.

When I'd climbed the mountain and found the top was flat,
I threw away ambition. I'd no more need of that.
I lost my love of beauty in colors bright and gay,
Shredded in the briers and the brambles on the way.
To ease the load of living I cast out love and grief.
Naked in the springtime,
I stand without a leaf.

Of Kings and Courage

I painted a picture of kings and of courage,
And there was your face, the foremost of all,
But you are the weakest of purpose, the meekest,
But somehow, I paint you as strong, straight, and tall.

I painted a picture of angels and sweetness,
And there you were, haloed and clad all in light.
I painted you gentle and soft, smiling sweetly,
But you are as like that as black is to white.

Then what am I seeing as I blend my colors?
Your true self that's hidden to all but to me?
Or am I just seeing my thoughts of a being,
And painting it just as I wish it to be?

With Only Wonder

I had no sign or sense of sound before.
All that I was, or lived, or breathed was pain.
And now that love has come and gone again,
Thoughts that are mine turn inward and explore
With searching fingers where love is no more,
Where tears no more are burning, drenching rain,
Where only numbness marks where dreams were slain,
And my slow heart is steady as before.

There is no pain left in me, no regret,
No mutiny, no wishful thought, no will.
It does seem strange that I should stand and let
Love go while eyes with only wonder fill ...
That I should love and lose again, and yet
That I can hear my slow heart, steady still.

Do Not Dream Back

Last night I dreamt that I went back once more
And through a veil of mist and sweet perfume
I saw the lilacs, lilacs all in bloom,
A fragrant bower of blossoms by the door.
Then I awakened, and my heart was sore.
There were no lilacs in my empty room.
The dead past crept again into its tomb …

Last night I dreamt that I went back once more.
Do not go back, for there is not a sky
To stem the tides of time, the point of pain.
Do not go back, for lilacs only die,
And tendrils twine and tangle in the lane.
Do not dream back to waken with a sigh.
For lilacs will not bloom again …
For lilacs will not bloom again …

———

Ghost Child's Face

I was just a wee, lame child ... pressed against a window.
You glanced at me and glanced away and stumbled through the night.
Your arms were full of bundles, and you did not wish to see
That cold sat at my left hand and hunger at my right.
And snow fell there
Upon the square,
A crown of jewels
For my hair.

I was just a wee, lame child, pressed against a window.
My hands were numb, my feet were numb, my heart too chill to warm.
At last released from cold-born dreams, I left a tiny figure
Pressed against a window, with its head upon its arm.
Snow drifted down,
A fleecy cloud,
To make a wee,
Lame child a shroud.

I was just a wee, lame child. Then you did not fear me.
If you would lose me now, you must lose conscience, or your goal
Will be hidden, ever hidden, by a wee, lame ghost-child's face,
Pressed against and peering in the windows of your soul.
Not all the suns
That ever shine
Can make your heart
Less chill than mine.

Shadow - Bond

I sit upon the garden wall, straight, and oh, so prim,
And watch my shadow stretch before, long and still, and slim.
How I should love to startle it to life upon the grass
And lose it from my dancing feet, a laughing fairy lass.
But fastened to my silver heels my shadow is, and I
Must sit sedately on the wall, and watch my roses die.

You come along the garden path, and to the garden wall.
There I watch my shadow lengthening and growing slim and tall.
You bear a question on your lips, a question and a sigh.
I know that I must answer it, and I must tell you why ...
Why we can't walk a shining path ... a straight clear path together,
Why I must haunt a garden wall and watch my roses wither.

But can I say that in a wood ... a haunted wood ... I heard
A nameless something call my name, a softly whispered word,
And I must hold this garden wall against a thousand morns,
Until I wound my shadow self, or tangle it in thorns,
Or can I say that life is sad and never will be sweet
'Til I lose my mortal shadow from a pair of fairy feet?

You bear a question on your lips ... a question and a sigh.
I know that I must answer it, and I must tell you why ...
Why I must haunt this garden wall from sun to shining sun
While roses wither, die and fall in petals one by one.
Until my shadow conquers me, my fairy story closes,
I'll ever hear a whispering among my dying roses.

What Broke Then?

It was but natural that he should feel
Such restlessness as nations great do sway,
Or makes a small boy, scornful, from his way
Kick pebbles with a dusty, stone-bruised heel.
'Twas but a space ago life did reveal
The glorious, the splendid, and the gay,
And with bright fingers streaked across the gray
A gaudy sun of power to which to kneel.

I heard a sound of breaking as the cup
Of power in his clutched fingers fell apart,
The slender crystal goblet with the sup
Of gods. I know I saw him pale and start,
With, "What broke then?" as he looked down, then up
From bleeding fingers and a shattered heart.

The Last Whip-Poor-Will

Although the shadows point a tracing finger
Along the path to home, to yon far hill,
To reach into the stars, I fain would linger
For the last cry of the last whip-poor-will,

And though his throbbing music is an anthem
Of poignant sorrow to a pain-filled night …
I shall look once more toward your window
For one last charm to carry of delight.

One glimpse, then out into a night of sorrow …
One glimpse to heal my wounds … but, oh, the scars
I carry down the path, knee deep in shadows
And up the hill, and out into the stars …

Bittersweet

I cannot weep today. I cannot weep,
For I still have so much of you to keep.
The little things you did, the things you said,
And how the moon was dim that summer night,
The way you smiled at me and bent your head …
Oh, I shall treasure these and keep them bright!
I still have, oh, so much of you to keep,
I cannot weep today. I cannot weep.

I cannot smile today. I cannot smile.
Love only lived for such a little while.
And, oh, to think I'll never know again
The beauty of a dim moon lacing trees,
The bittersweet of love … a sudden pain,
Crying out and dying on the breeze.
Love only lived for such a little while.
I cannot smile today. I cannot smile.

———————

WAR AND CONFLICT

*Aola's brother, Jimmy Seery and Bill
WW II England – 1944*

If You Should Go to Fight

If you should go to fight, away from me,
Though it be across the ocean wild and wide,
My soul would cross the world, the wildest sea,
To march beside you, always at your side.

If you should go to fight, my dear, away,
I would be beside you then, as I am now.
If you should wounded fall one bitter day,
My soothing hand would cool your fevered brow.

If you should go to fight, my dear, and die,
In a strange and unknown land away from me,
Then I would come there to you where you'd lie,
And make another grave beside for me.

If you should go to fight, my dear, then all
The life that I have here for me would cease.
Across the world there comes a far, faint call.
Let's kneel together here … and pray for peace.

Don't Let Your Heart Go South

Don't let your heart go south, young man
Or you will know defeat,
For North is North and South is South,
The twain will never meet.

The North and South will woo the West
Alack and well-a-day.
You'll find you wore your best blue vest,
And she preferred the gray.

The war was fought and never won.
The South will all agree.
Scratch any Southern gentleman,
And you will scratch a Lee.

Kiss any pretty Southern miss
And whisper pretty words.
Ghosts in gray will twist and turn
And clank their rusty swords.

An Empire Falls

The Death Wind's voice is hollow in the trees,
The trees that shiver bleakly, prophecy
Decadence of an empire, bloody wars
To tear the tops of buildings from the sky.
The Death Mist rises ghostlike from the plain
And heralds fall of empire, fall of man …

To rise and fall and rise and fall again
As it has so done since the world began.
Death comes again with sharper, brighter sword,
And men forget that life and land are sweet,
And, eagerly, they gird their armor on
To the rhythm of a million marching feet.
The Death Wind's voice says, hollow in the trees,
"The patriot's fire is mockery, a lie!"
And blackened, twisted, sharp against the blue,
The trees that shiver, bleakly prophecy.

Leopold

The King was in his counting house that day.
One and one and two. One and one and two.
He counted as the gold coins filtered through
   The pale white hands he folded as to pray.
The King was in the counting house that day.
His soldiers fought for him as brave men do.
One and one and two. One and one and two,
   They fell to brave another, darker way.

While brave men go to war, and women weep,
   A King must drink of power, a poison brew.
   How can he close his eyes, or ever sleep?
   Oh, Traitor, this the curse we set on you,
That you may ever count your poor lost sheep,
One and one and two. One and one and two.

Hold Hard to All Good Things

   Not being very young, how can I say
When hearts of youth are drowning in defeat,
   That Taps will know again a Reveille,
And youth will dawn as brave again, as sweet.

   Not being very young, what can I say
   When all of youth is savoring its sorrow,
When there are partings, there are tears today,
   When there is not, in certainty, a morrow.

Not being very young, but yet to know
The twilight's scented mist, the brushing wing
Of promises that on young faces blow
When it is night, and it is still, and spring …

Not being very young, but holding close
Out of the long ago an April rain,
A gentle sound no martial strain can still,
The sweet of love, the poignancy of pain …

I have but this to say, hold close today …
The world will never be quite young again.

Lend Lease

Here is a seed. Please take this seed and plant it.
Love-tend this seed and let it bloom and grow,
And as it grows, remember that I sent it,
But it belongs to him who chose to sow.
No charity is this, no idle giving,
The seed is God's … it is not mine to give.
In bringing it to life, you do the giving,
And if you make it grow and bloom and live,
Then we will have a bond that makes us brothers.
Here is the source of every human need.
When harvesting, pass some seed on to others.
This is the seed of Peace.
Please plant this seed.

The Right to Bear Arms

I don't like guns!
Yet I would not deny
Young Nimrod, with eager eagle eye,
His right to bear the birthright of our sons,

A citizen,
To hold against his cheek
The walnut butt, love-polished, and to seek
Rapport with men,

With men who stalk
Our forests, fierce and tall,
Divested of the things that make men small
Because they walk

With ancient laws.
The time will come again,
And we will have an urgent need of men,
Unfilled, because

I don't like guns.

———————

I Sat Upon a Quiet Hill

I sat upon a quiet hill at close of day,
And watched a maple in her autumn glory sway,
And as her bright leaves caught the golden sun
And drifted earthward slowly, one by one,
I watched them fall and somehow seemed to know
That was the way that man was meant to go,
To go in glory from Life's golden crown,
Into the Winter's sleep go drifting down,
And leave behind, to linger 'gainst the gray,
A memory to light the winter day.

I sat upon a quiet hill at close of day,
And watched a maple in her autumn glory sway.
And as I watched, the cannon oversea
Spoke in a thunderous tongue that shook the tree.
Ten million guns cried out! Ten million jeers
That made the leaves rain down like golden tears.
Aye. Go in glory from Life's golden crown.
Into the winter's sleep go drifting down.
But I saw the slow sun sink in ruddy flood
And saw the late leaves fall like drops of blood.

Again

Time is healing that great, gaping wound,
Inflicted by the man-made thing that we call war,
And echoes of the thing that shook the earth
Are fast becoming legendary lore,
But I remember groping in the dark,
And mud and filth and rats and fog and stench,
And the weariness of waiting for the world
To end this war, release me from my trench,
But I've learned since …
'Tis ever thus …

That black is white
And wrong is right,
And so, I go
Again to fight.

A Mother's Vigil

Sleep, my little one, here in my arms.
The stars are out, and the night is old.
Here you are warm, but over the sea
The stars are blind, and the earth is cold.

Sleep, my little one. The darkness heals.
A soft warm wind steals out of the night,
But winds are bitter in France tonight,
And the great shells burst in splintered light.

Sleep, my little one. In baby's eyes
I forget my woes, and in his hair.
But the beating of drums is on the breeze,
And the marching of feet somewhere ... somewhere.

Sleep, my baby ... so kind is sleep ...
As I through the night my vigil keep,
And Mother will watch as baby dreams ...
Watch and weep ... wait and weep.

War

Forward and march. Forward and march ...
Oh, brother across the sea.
Aye, close your eyes to the marching lines
That flaunt reality.

Shoulder your arms. Shoulder your arms ...
For a king or for a queen.
Into the dawn, a dealer of death,
An effortless machine.

Blood and war ... war and blood
Into a robot's brain.
And who shall say who is the one
To wear the cross of Cain!

Thirst

There's a murder in the mountain
And the mesa's Devil-haunted.
I am chilling with the hot sun,
I am fevered with the cold,
   And my straining brain is burdened
    For my saddlebags are laden,
   Filled to overflowing with
       a
         dead
           man's
             gold.

There are shadows in the shallows
And the depths of Poison River.
 There are buzzards swooping slowly
 After something in the sand.
  Could it be its shade they're seeking,
  Or a drink from Poison River,
  Or a gold coin glittering in
       a
         dead
           man's
             Hand?

There's no water in the desert.
Many miles to Broken Arrow.
It is further still to Paris,
And I haven't got a boat…
Drink your wine, you thirsty Frenchmen!
There is blood in Poison River,
And these gold coins rattle in
a
man's
dry
Throat!

God's Child

Little Boy saw so many tears
In this world of sighs and woe,
That he shut his eyes to the passing years,
And his small world ceased to grow.

Little Boy heard so many sighs
That he shut them out with joy.
Though cannon thundered and kingdom's fell,
He was a little boy.

Little Boy wanted to go to war
And hear the drums. Where some
Could see grim Death march in the ranks,
He saw a bright, red drum.

Little Boy grew up straight and tall,
Though time for him stood still,
And all the townsfolk pitied him,
Alone atop a hill.

Then twilight came. An old, old man
Who clasped some foolish toy,
Lay strangely still. I came and wept …
And saw a little boy.

Two Mothers

I have come to the dimness of this little church
And knelt me down, Mary, to pray,
For we are both Mothers, and you understand …
And today is Easter Day.

The world darkens now as it did once for you,
And war clouds cast gloom on my heart,
And I know now that Mary, the mother of Him,
And I are not far apart.

The marching of feet and the beating of drums,
And a lad standing tall, brave and slim,
And I know now the sorrow, the pain in your heart …
The pain that you felt for Him.

But when the time comes, and he marches away,
And if marked by the fates he should go …
Then, for me, go weep o'er his little white cross
As you did o'er a cross long ago.

Who Goes There?

The sentry, waking from the drowsy spell
That comes with shadows, and with the breathless hush
That portends night, stood listening in the gloom.
Too young he was to have to watch the field
Where night, with shadow fingers traced old names
On crosses in stiff whiteness, row on row.
Where crosses filed like armies down the plain
And folded shadow-hands on mounds before.
Too young he was to have to watch the field,
With his new uniform and his new dreams,
A marching song still ringing in his ears,
A victory song that lived against the night,
'Til through the sullen silence came the sound.

"Who goes there!"
He asked it quietly, but yet he knew
That there would be no answer. There was none.
For through his song of victory came a sound
Of marching feet, but dragging, stiff, and slow …
To the same words and tune, but off a beat,
Mechanical, invincible, and slow …
The frosted frozen grasses spoke with sound
Of feet that passed, but did not bow before
The sudden wind that shivered in the sky
And snapped a bough, ice-laden, with a sigh.

"Who goes there!"
Back of the song, there came another song,
So different, but yet so much the same …
As shadow feet marched on, impassively,
Dim against the nearer sounds of music,
But slower, still, and twice as passionless.
And somewhere, back of sounds and silences,
Time faded into time. Year into year.
The victory, the dirge, the lagging march
With the undertones that made each full note round,
Swept on into a symphony of sound.

"Who goes there!"
The boy put down his gun, and leaned against
A monument of marble, no more chill
Than he, with all the things which he had seen.
The music changed its time. It's like a hymn,
The sentry thought … a hymn that's sung with tears.
And stumbling 'cross the field, and up the path,
A white robed figure walked, bowed down with pain …
To set his cross among the crosses there.
The white robed figure turned. His glory grew.
The sentry knelt in wonder, asking … "Who …
Who goes there?"

The Name of Spain

The mountain split asunder. Down rolled his craggy head.
Down into the valley land, to lie among the dead.
An echo caught the dying cries, echoed the cannons roar,
And sent it thundering through the skies to sound from shore to shore,
All mingled with a woman's cries, "God let there be no war!"

Wilt to end the wind, Oh, flag of shame! All love for thee is dead!
Drowned within a pool of blood, by such a tyrant led!
Should I to fight my brother, go in quest of worldwide fame
And pay the price of self and soul coaxed by the cannon's flame?
God lay thy hand upon this globe and purge the name of Spain.

***** Aola Seery, published at age 17,
Golden Harvest, Mistletoe Press, 1937*****

Peacemaker

I wonder, Stephen Foster, as you lie
Dreaming of Jeanie with the light brown hair,
If you remember anguish and despair
There where the grasses whisper to the sky.
For we recall, with eyes that are not dry,
As we come, reverent pilgrims to you there
Where vibrant songs still tremble in the air
Though fiddle and old bow are hanging high,
That once you taught a nation sympathy,
And sang of South to North, and North to South,
Brought tears to eyes that could not, would not see,
Where there had been, too long, a bitter drought.
The grasses here will murmur constantly
The songs of peace and love that knew your mouth.

The Shadow Place

They met unmasked within the shadow place,
One with a gaunt and craggy, homely face,
The other, slim and sad-eyed, mannerly,
Of princely mien, of gentleman's degree.
They met together on a common ground
And spoke together where there is no sound.

Behind the one a drifting shadow breeze
Played vagrantly in gnarled, Ohio trees
About a log-built cabin on a morn
Of dew and morning glory tangled thorn.

Behind the other sang a darker wind,
In lace-plumed trees to move and touch and find
The scent of jasmine and to breathe and sigh
Against white colonnades that touched the sky.

The two men spoke of home and homely things,
And who would ever know that both were kings.
And in a word or two without pretense,
They settled and discarded difference.

For in this silent place a silent word
Has more power than a shield, more than a sword.
Peace touched the portal with a dove's white feather.
The gates swung wide, and they went in together.

Independence Day

On our day of independence, Independence Day,
I rose in the morning and the dawn was sweet,
Just as the moon and the stars went away,
And I set a flag 'twixt the house and the street,
And the red was redder than blood could be,
And the blue was bluer than any sea,
And the whiteness glowed in its purity,
On our day of independence, Independence Day.

I listened to the news in the afternoon
Of a war that raged across a world half-way,
Of a war that raged to the strident tone
Of cannon and the sound of a marching tune.
Oh, mobilization and death and blood
Sounded to the beat of the war-drums thud,
And flags of freedom trampled in the mud,
On our day of independence, Independence Day.

I watched little children as the dusk came down,
With their fireworks flaming as the sky grew gray,
Watched a drift of stars burst above the town,
And a red frame of light flame behind the town.
I stayed up for hours and looked at the sight,
Then folded the red, the blue, and the white.
Then I went in the house and cried all night,
On our day of independence, Independence Day.

Dictator

I hate these thoughts,
These strange, inconsequential things
That flit from nowhere into nowhere in my head,
For this I know,
I could be great
Were they but dead.

This, too, I know,
That I must strive
Toward one single purpose constantly,
For only thus
I can be what
I want to be.

I must aside
Put dreams, ideals and such I've left from youth,
Fool this land and rule this land I've trod,
For now I see
My destiny
Is playing God.

Czechoslovakia

I have a son.
A tall son,
A strong son,
And a brave one.
When war came as a great dark cloud,
Threatening our homes
And our lives,
And our country,
He said,
"Mother, I shall go to be a soldier."
And so it was.
And war came on as a great dark cloud.
In my mind I saw him
Lying in a trench in death, or perhaps
Calling for his mother,
And so I prayed for peace.
Today, I saw him, with a bundle on his shoulders,
Bereft of home and God and all that meant his soul,
Stumbling in search of a place to exist.
And this is the peace I prayed for
In preference to Death.
Forgive me,
My son.

Holland, May 14th, 1940

Why do you sit beside the window there?
The house is full of idleness. Before
You would have knelt outside the cottage door
And scoured the threshold clean and white and bare,
But not today. The fields surrounding wear
Black bayonets of trees, and there are four
Tall windmills wheeling still, and all the roar
Has gone and left unhealed the shattered air.
Why do you sit beside the window still?
You must not weep for white doves that have flown.
You must arise and scour the threshold 'til
You wash away the blood that stains the stone
And does not wash away, and never will,
A stain not sand nor ashes may atone.

You must arise and care for, tenderly,
Poor trampled tulips. Touch them with a sigh.
They made a couch whereon your dead might lie,
And there were dead, from cities to the sea.
Oh, what is death, and what is liberty?
Arise and go without. The raveled sky
Is placid blue and soundless. Not a cry
Strikes out to break its bright tranquility.
There's nothing but the memory of tears
To haze the flawless blue or mar the day.
The building of a people all these years,
All Holland's dykes have broken, given way,
And swept her with a flood of blood and tears …
An epitaph for Holland … and its May!

Trampled Dreams

The leaves are turning
As the year begins to turn,
And the stars swing into new courses.
The earth and the air are stirred with new promises,
And dreams are being dreamt.

We are all dreamers,
The lowliest of us,
The holiest of us ...
The richest, the poorest,
Those who go their way singing,
Those who go their way sighing.
We all go dreaming our dreams,
And with our eyes toward the horizon.

Careful, Dreamer,
Yours is a great responsibility.
On your shoulders rest the burdens of the world.
You had a dream of America,
A dream of liberty and justice,
The beautiful simplicity of liberty and justice.
You founded your dreams on truth and love,
And through God's grace, you built it.

The leaves are turning
As the year begins to turn
This sad year, leaving bloody footprints
In its wake. Across the seas, they have no dreams,
Save those, perhaps, of dreams to rule the world.
They have no dreams.
They only know reality,
That, but as they see it.

And these are men, and these are nations men have dreamt,
Men with codes and creeds and faith in some one thing.
Yes, these are men ... accomplices of death,
Who trample flags and faith and such into the mire,
And walk where men are bidden not to go.

Duel in Simmon's Swamp

Bill and I went down to the swamp to kill a devil,
Down to Simmon's Swamp where the vapors hiss.
Bill took a rabbit's foot to ward off evil.
I took the mem'ry of my true love's kiss.

Bill knew I'd fall
    When the fight begun.
        He said, "I'll tell
            Your mother, Son."

Through the dank, black bog we went to kill a devil,
'Cause there's no peace 'til a devil's dead.
I took a long knife, as slim as a needle,
But Bill took an axe with a double head.

Bill knew I'd fall
    'Cause I couldn't run.
        He said, "I'll tell
            Your true love, Son."

So, there in the marsh-muck, we fought to kill a devil,
Bill's axe weighing twenty pound. My blade was slim,
But my true love's kiss scorned the devil's evil ...
And the moon struck my blade and blinded him.

The devil's dead ...
    But the price was life.
        I go, alone,
            To tell Bill's wife.

Valentines Day – 1918

It's strange to think of paper hearts and lace
Where dark skies flame and dim and flame and dim,
But somehow, I can almost see your face
And hear your sweet voice saying … trust in Him …
And so, I send this poor scrawled note of mine
To serve, in its poor way … a valentine.

But once I sent you paper hearts and lace
And sang a love song to your two sweet eyes,
But now I sing a new song in its place …
A song that says that true love never dies,
But glows a steady flame 'gainst sorrows breath …
And goes … a diving lantern unto death.

But about love's pale, tall candle in the night,
The whole earth shudders with the bursting shell,
And skies careen in slanting, splintered light …
But those are things I didn't mean to tell.
Let this note that I love you be a sign,
And serve in its poor way … a valentine.

Comrade Unremembered

Do you remember me?
I was beside you when you went to war
All clad in shaggy skins. I saw you go
Armed with a sharpened stone, beat down your foe …
Another browless beast … and neither know
A mercy or a qualm in doing so.

You should remember me,
For we have marched so many, many times
In places where the blood ran deep, so deep,
The flower of a war-torn world to reap,
And ever you forgot from war to war
You had been touched by Death and felt His sleep.

You don't remember me …
Yet we tramped side by side at Brandywine.
At Gettysburg we were together, too,
And No Man's Land. Remember, I met you …
We stopped to speak, halfway between the lines,
You had a message … never got it through.

You should remember Death!
For now, we are about to march again,
For you forgot your dying cry, your plea,
That peace and love eternal reign, so we
Shall go again to war, and I shall claim
My share of fools, for fools ye mortals be!

The Grandeur of Spain

Faith and its glory are hidden from sight
By the darkness of night and the fog of despair.
Above the loud cannon flit shades of the night
To hover and cover shamed flags once so fair.
Oh, Brother, such sadness!
Ah, Mother, the woe.
Bright rockets for sunlight, the cruel shell for rain.
The day passes quickly, but night goes so slow,
And gone is the glory,
The grandeur of Spain.

Ahead lie the trenches like treacherous wells.
There lies my brother. Hark! This is the hour!
And out of the darkness a bugle call swells,
And calls me against him, my family's flower.
Oh, Brother such sadness!
Ah, Mother, the woe!
Will dawn ever come in its splendor again?
The day passes quickly but night goes so slow,
And gone is the glory,
The grandeur of Spain.

*****Aola Seery, published at age 17,*
Golden Harvest, Mistletoe Press, 1937****

The Confederate

He tried to stop the wind,
The northern wind,
That spread a killing chill across his land,
And he forged himself a sword of tempered steel,
Forged in the fires of faith, to fit his hand.
No ordinary sword was this, but one
Made of the southern blood, the warm dark moon,
Trees blurred with mossy lace, white colonnades,
The sun in morning-gloried corn at noon.

And rode to stop the wind, the wind that blew
The breath of Death on everything he knew
And understood,
And in his way was true
Both to himself, and to his country's word …
A gallant man, a soldier with a sword,
A sword too heavy for one man to wield,
Sad soldier with a sword
Without a shield.

They say today, in some dark swamp land's sleep,
While men in far off countries die and bleed,
Excalibur lies hidden, buried deep,
Its haft to hand if there should be a need.
Dear God, if there is need for us to wield
The sword of honor, let us wear a shield.
The courage of conviction, bright, undimmed,
Can't stop the wind.

Every Day at Sundown

Every day at sundown, a mother kneels and prays.
Every day at sundown, the day's last sunbeam plays
Upon her rapt and shining face, illumining her hair,
But no one sees her kneeling, save the silent watcher there.

Monuments

The fifes came shrilling over hill,
And drums beat down the dell.
They broke a million brave men's wills,
And drummed them all to Hell.

They broke a million mothers' hearts,
And in the sun's last glow,
A million tears fall on the graves
Where poppies bleed and blow.

Shadow pictures, marching brave,
Shadows dying … lone.
Mothers weeping by a grave
In Arlington … Unknown.

Mary, Mother, in that day
Of triumph and of joy,
Let all these mothers find that he …
The Unknown … is their boy.

Cycle

I saw the soldiers marching,
Marching to the fray,
Going forth to battle,
Nonchalant and gay.

Then, as I stepped among the crowd,
The better so to see,
One waved and smiled, another bowed.
A bold one winked at me.

I saw the soldiers marching,
Home from across the sea.
The one who winked before was blind,
And one I did not see.

I watched my roses fade and fall
And wondered with a sigh
Why all things beautiful must fade,
And all things brave must die.

*****Aola Seery, published at age 17,
Golden Harvest, Mistletoe Press, 1937*****

Rain

I saw red rain in Shanghai, on ashes in the dust,
Bloody sabers slashing where a thousand smokes arose,
Red rain falling sullen on the smoking ruins of Hell,
On idols charred and broken as a day burned to its close.

I saw red rain in Shanghai, and I shuddered at the sight,
A dragon wounded to the death and dying in the mud.
Bloody sabers slashing in a soft deceptive night.
A nation weeping on the shores of rivers running blood.

Then silver mist in England. It swept across the moor,
Drowning purple heather and weeping silver tears.
A cold sad face is England's, through a dripping, shining veil,
Where comes no light, and comes no sun, and not a sound one hears.

Bitter tears are England's, like tears above a grave,
A pale wan woman weeping where the face of Death is seen.
I knew the sorrow in me there, and though there came no sun,
I knew the mist upon my face and was so clean…so clean.

But give me rain in April in a lilac scented dawn,
When the ground is greening over, and the trees are new again.
For my heart is young with April, and my heart is new with spring,
Dreaming in the winter, to be wakened with the rain.

I saw red rain in Shanghai, on ashes in the dust,
And sorrow lived in England, with tears upon its wings.
But give me rain in April on a freshened country lane …
My heart is born anew in rain with all these lovely things.

John Smith – 1880 to 1929

Here lies John.
He went away to war when first he heard
The call for men, and not a word
Spoke he of fear, nor did we see
The coward in his face, but silently
He put his desk in order … 'twas his way
To do so at the end of every day …
And kissed his wife goodbye, went marching on.
Here lies John.

John came home,
But not among the wounded and the dead.
"The bravest man," the captain said,
"I ever saw." He saw the war
Just as a job to do, and wounded sore,
Wrote out his will and put it on a shelf,
To save the postage, took it home himself,
And no one knew he had braved death alone.
John came home.

Here lies John.
He came home, stacked the papers that he found
And bought up stocks he thought were sound.
But being John, and being neat,
When all the evening papers screamed defeat,
He smoothed his desk and ended with his hand
The life which he so orderly had planned.
Here, 'neath this plain, but well kept, strip of lawn,
Here lies John.

BROTHERHOOD

Aola, dressed in Northern Plains Native American ceremonial dress belonging to a friend, a Cheyenne princess. Oklahoma, 1943

To Whom It May Concern

How big is your heart?
Have you seen these?

Low hovels built from tin and scraps and cardboard
Squatting in a tin-can-littered Hell
Where slow death crawls and with impartial finger
Lays hand on old and young and sick and well;
Dull heat, and babes inert and sick with hunger,
Swelled throats and parched dry lips that dream of ice.
Death lies in eyes that vainly seek for shadow,
And cracked red earth and hot sun must suffice;
Strong men whose bodies and whose minds are twisted
Upon the lathe of life, and worn too thin,
And women who sit stupid by the bedsides
Of their children, and watch slow death creeping in?

Or have you seen low hovels in a snowstorm
Or starving bodies lean against the wind
Like lean-ribbed foolish cattle in a blizzard,
With burlap, rags and papers 'round them pinned?
Have you ever cowered foodless in a corner
While the wind brings in pneumonia where you lie,
And with purple face, and pinched, cold-brittle fingers
Wait, and weep, and plead and pray to die?

Have you seen these?
How big is your heart?

———

Color Line

When I first saw your face, I only saw
Your soul upon it, not the color of it.
Knowing you again, my friend, I love it.
What matters color? Race? God didn't draw
A color-line, nor did He put by law
Your race to serving mine, nor mine above it.
He took perfection, and divided it, and of it
Gave equally. Yours is not every flaw.
He gave to you the power of poetry,
Love of beauty, and the love of light.
In your music is the pulsing mystery
Of tom-toms throbbing death-songs through the night.
While I am friend to you, and you to me,
What matters it that you are black, I white?

One God

I saw two little children
As I passed through the town.
One had cheeks as white as milk
And tumbled hair as soft as silk,
A shining, golden crown.

I saw two little children,
As I passed down the street.
One had tiny ebon curls,
A dark-skinned face and teeth like pearls,
And laughter shrill and sweet.

I saw two little children
And that was all I knew.
One was black and one was white,
One like day and one like night,
Knew this ... and there were two.

I saw two little children
In laughing innocence,
And I saw each little one
Had caught a portion of the sun.
There was no difference.

Two laughing little children,
The day they spent in play,
And one was black, and one was white,
But each knelt at home at night
With one God to whom to pray

White Mist Rising

Broken bits of flint, you tell a story
That man's lips have forgotten many years.
You mark the graves of unremembered glory.
You lie along the quiet Trail of Tears.

You lie beside the length of some dead chieftain
The busy world has long since ceased to mourn.
You lie against some quiet country hillside.
You crowd the roots of growing Indian corn.

Who knows? Perhaps the dead chiefs will arise,
And gathering their arrowheads once more,
With a dark look of remembrance in their eyes,
Will paint their bodies once again for war.

And then there will be weeping in the valley,
And white mist rising, rising on the hill.
Ghost buffalo will thunder on the mesa
'Till echoes die, and all is still ... so still.

Then tom-toms will pound out across the silence,
'Till all the earth is shaken with the sound,
And the Indian with his vengeance will go singing,
At last, to see his happy hunting ground.

Indian Maid

When last we lived, I saw you riding, riding,
All clad in shining armor, bright array,
In the gallant troops of soldier Coronado,
I remember how I thrilled to hear you say,
"I love you, Indian maid of Oklahoma" ...
For my heart your foreign tongue could understand.
But the Spaniard spoke with two tongues and returned
To a señorita in another land.

Had you returned, you would have found the Red Bud
Had flowered into scarlet with the stain
Of a brokenhearted Indian maiden's lifeblood,
As her true love went a-sailing off to Spain.
This is my answer to you when you ask me
Why we can't love, the reason we must part ...
I've carried through two lives, two long, long ages
The pain and sorrow of a broken heart.
You live from life to life, but I am haunted
By life and life, in one long endless chain.
I've felt the same old sorrow endless ages,
As each time you've gone sailing back to Spain.

Desecration

Come with me and kneel with me.
There's no one left to mourn him.
He was laid where he fell on the battlefield
And they built a mossy mound.
He was laid to rest with his bow beside
And feathers to adorn him.
Then the white men drove away his sons
And plowed his resting ground.
The winds were left to sigh for him
And the clouds to do his weeping.
The sky is his teepee of royal blue
To shelter and shade his grave.

The mockingbird sings a lullaby
As the chieftain lies a-sleeping.
There's none to mourn but nature
But nature tends her brave.
The clouds do weep, and the winds do sigh.
All nature is a-crying.
His race has lost its god, its pride
And turned to white man's ways.
He's buried on a white man's land,
'Neith a white man's grain he's lying,
And the breezes mourn as the Indian corn
Above the Indian sways.

———

Cherokee Prophecy

Like a sentinel he stood
On a rugged mountain crest
With the sun's last upflung rays
Playing on his beaded vest ...
A symbol of a vanished race,
An outcast from his native home,
He raised aloft his arms in prayer
To the great White Spirit's throne.

"Father, hear me while I speak ...
Speak the words that hurt me so.
Shall we perish from this earth,
Like the mighty buffalo?
Shall we wander on and on,
Driven by the white man's hand?
Like the mighty wasteland wind
Drives the helpless desert sand?

"Father of my ancient race,
Paint upon yon darkening sky ...
Paint a comet's flaming path,
As a sign we shall not die.
Lead us to our future home
Where the buffalo abound.
Guide your humble children's steps
To that happy hunting ground."

Then in answer to his prayer,
A comet, dressed in flaming robe,
Sailed across the starlit sky ...
Pointed to his last abode ...
Pointed to the Trail of Tears ...
Pointed with a flaming hand ...
Burst and faded in the night
Over Oklahoma land.

Because Someone Did Not Forget

Out in the haunted prairie lands,
The ghosts of the past are walking,
And grasses shudder and fill the night
With the whisper of their talking,
And the brown owl cries his lonely cry
To the eerie gloom of a haunted sky.
Here the ghosts of the past are met ...
Because someone did not forget.

Out on the haunted trail tonight,
Where a pall of darkness hovers,
Riders come from who knows where
To greet their living brothers ...
And a sound comes back like a sad wind's sigh
As a faint halloo rings 'cross the sky.
Here the ghosts of the past are met ...
Because someone did not forget.

The past comes back so easily
If only one remembers
Forgotten faces seen across
A campfire's dying embers ...
Campfires blazing, burning low,
As campfires did so long ago.
Here the ghosts of the past are met ...
One can't forget ... cannot forget.

———

To a Tom Tom

Mute and silent you are hanging,
Yet I hear your rhythm beat
Through the stillness of the forest
With a fiery, savage heat,
And the very forest quivers with the sound
And holds its breath.
Death! The word comes sounding, pounding,
Death! Death! Death!

Death to those who steal the forest.
Sullen is their dusky song.
You have stolen, killed and plundered,
You have burdened us with wrong,
Made the warriors work like women,
Made them weep and ruined their will,
Kill! The word comes singing, ringing,
Kill! Kill! Kill!

Mute and silent you are hanging,
Yet I hear your rhythm beat
Since long ago the Indian
Bent the knee at white man's feet,
And the graves of those old warriors
Have been touched by sun and frost.
Lost! The word comes throbbing, sobbing,
Lost! Lost! Lost!

Little Papoose

Little Papoose, the last of the Chieftains,
Out on the dry plains, the night winds are sighing.
The Lodge of the Sun has been long ago leveled,
The skulls of the buffalo, bleaching and drying,
Where hooves shook the prairie in echoing thunder,
Are buried by plowshares that turn them in under.

Little Papoose, the last of the Chieftains,
This is the evening, and the shadows are falling.
You will hear whispers from out of the darkness,
The voice of your people keeps calling and calling.
The mockingbird's song, and the brown owl's soft sorrow
Are commands you must follow. Remember tomorrow!

Little Papoose, the last of the Chieftains,
The last of the sacred fires ceases its burning.
The stones will be hard 'neath your moccasined feet,
And the trail will be long and with many a turning.
The Indian will follow the white flag of truce.
Go guided by lightning, Little Papoose.

———

The Eagle and the Dove

They have clipped your wings, oh eagle of the earth,
And you now know white man's tears and white man's mirth,
And you, perhaps, forget you ever knew
That skies could be so shining and so blue …
Have bartered all the glory of your dawn,
And your stars for nights that false stars shine upon.
I, with almost sadness see you now,
Wings clipped, and bound, and fashioned to the plow.
"The world is small, so small," the fates do say,
"And even reigns of eagles pass away."

They have clipped your wings, but other dusky eyes,
The replicas of those that knew the skies,
Look out from paler faces, with the tale
Of a march with Death as leader, down a trail.
Those hands which may have placed a lodge-pole higher,
Have now built cities out of smoke and fire …
Chains have been formed of strength and forged of love
Through this meeting of the eagle and the dove …
Though eagles may have clipped and broken wings,
They reign in this, the greater scheme of things.

Trail of Tears

There is a trail all silver with the moon
And undimmed with all the passing of the years,
With shadows sent from within their graves to haunt
And mourn in silence o'er the Trail of Tears.

Shades of warriors from Death's lodges sent,
Tall as birches and like the birches, slim,
Sent to avenge a father, brother, son,
Dark eyes burning, faces once calm, grim.

With soundless voice, they sadly tell their tale,
How the white men came and of the woe he brought,
How his mansions built from brick and shining stone,
With flesh and blood from them were dearly bought.

They who were once the kings upon the earth
Are doomed to sorrow ceaseless through the years,
And silently with eyes long dry they ride,
The guardians of the Trail of Tears.

*****Aola Seery, published at age 17,
Golden Harvest, Mistletoe Press, 1937*****

Cliff Dwelling

Why should I, who have known paneled walls,
Feel here at home in this small earthen cell,
Carved in red-brown cliffs with red-brown hands
And left behind. Here ghosts and spirits dwell.

I speak not, for it seems I should not tell
That I walk to this corner wondering whether
A wind voice spoke, or memory's eerie bell
Told me that here I'd find one lone blue feather.

Singing Bird

Indian maiden, Singing Bird,
I know that I am growing old.
The world is growing strange to me ...
A little strange, a little cold,
And in the twilight I have heard
You calling me, oh, Singing Bird.

We knew the wild free prairie land,
The freedom of the hills and sky
Until the white man bound our wings,
The wild bird could no longer fly.
A caged bird pines and never sings,
And finds another way to wings.

But I, I learned the way of chains.
A chieftain cannot die, you know.
They put a fence across the plains,
And killed the mighty buffalo.
My people fought, in wrath and fear.
They would not hear me ... would not hear.

But now, I'm growing very old ...
I know that I shall join you there,
And I shall be a proud young chief,
And you a maid with dusky hair.
Your silver whisper I have heard,
Oh, Singing Bird ... Oh, Singing Bird.

**** Aola Seery, published at age 17,
Golden Harvest, Mistletoe Press, 1937****

NATURE

*Aola with her daughter, "Baby Jack,"
Getting a Ride by Aola's sister, Jackie*

Fall of the King

Oh, eerie world, how strange with light of death.
The summers gone. How swift the seasons roll!
And great white winter with his chilling breath
Bears on his wings of wind a feathered soul
That soared in merry flight on summer breeze
Ere great white winter walked among the trees.

Swift as the bird was, swifter was the wind,
A chilling bolt flying from the northern star
That malevolent watched the earth and darted in
When autumn left the seasons door ajar
And drove poor coward summer from the sky,
Drove she who left her little friend to die.

*****Aola Seery, published at age 17,
Golden Harvest, Mistletoe Press, 1937*****

This is the Sea

This is the sea, and I have stood beside it
And gazed into a great infinity.
I made a song of it and stood and cried it
To the small, unheeding world. This is the sea.

This is the sea, and in my strength is its strength …
And all its stormy self my being fills,
And in my eyes is all the depth of its length …
I, who borrowed strength from rugged hills.

This is the sea. I have sent cloudships sailing
Upon the masts, the banner of the sky,
And when my ships becalm and winds are failing,
I shall send them skimming onward with a sigh.

And I shall walk there, singing on the shore,
Wild and straight and slim and young and free,
And listen to the wild surf rise and roar.
This is the sea … this is the sea … the sea.

The Black Pony

A little black pony at midnight
Waits on the top of a hill,
One with the sky without moonlight,
And listens for the shrill
And wild, sweet notes of the fairy things
That people the scented night,
When the shadows are free to roam at will,
And the dark moon gives no light.

Then, right at the stroke of midnight,
The fairy folk appear,
And his flight o'er the dusky meadow
Is that of a frightened deer.
Silently over the meadow,
Swift down the silver grassed lane,
Wee riders with whispering laughter
Holdfast to his glossy black mane.

Snow

Snow.
Iridescent and sparkling bright and full of tiny rainbows
As the white gleam of the sun strikes its crystal surface
With a hard, almost metallic sound.

Snow.
Bitter chill and killing cold and howling like a demon,
Lashing spray before a wind sped from a blackened cloud,
Crushing life beneath its cruel palm.

Snow.
Lying in serenity, all cool and clean and peaceful.
Trees and old rail fences stand in lace-like silhouette
Against the moonlit purity of snow.

My Friend, Storm

I never cared for dogs before
Until that moment when he came,
Wet, half frozen, tired and sore,
Limping through the lashing rain.

I let him in and cleaned his wounds,
Fed him, dried him, made him warm,
And then he wagged his tail and grinned.
I petted him and named him Storm.

He loved me and I loved him, too.
Of all my friends he was the best
For few are tried, and few are true,
Here in this great, unfriendly west.

I'd hurry homeward when the sun
Had softened to a few faint gleams.
I knew I'd find when work was done,
One who would listen to my dreams.

Then one night when winds blew hard,
He disappeared into the gloam.
The winds had taken back their ward
The storm, once more, received its own.

Whip-Poor-Will

As soft as night, and softer still
Comes plaintive notes of whip-poor-will.
Perched in the great tree's sheltering shade,
A formless thing by eve's light made.
It would seem to one who heard,
A fairy rather than a bird.
A fairy thing content to trill
This melody ... whip-whip-poor-will.

*****Aola Seery, published at age 17,
Golden Harvest, Mistletoe Press, 1937*****

Enchanted Garden

Walk softly through my garden
Should you chance to come by day,
For my garden is enchanted.
You must tread the narrow way
Lest you trample on a cricket
And the birds should cease to sing,
Lest a clumsy, heavy mortal shoe
Should brush a fairy's wing.

Walk softly through my garden
Should you chance to come at eve
When the moon is busy tying
Golden clouds into a sheaf.
You might trample on a shadow
Lying trembling in the grass.
You might not kneel to see the queen,
The queen of fairies pass.

Walk softly through the garden
Until I shall come to you
Where a gnarled old pear stands pointing,
And the grass is wet with dew,
And I'll tell you of my willow.
She's a fairy in disguise
Who bends to touch her dainty foot …
Her long hair in her eyes.

And we'll walk through my garden,
And we'll find the gates ajar
And open wide on fairyland
Where the fairy beings are ...
Where a twisted tree will give you
Of the knowledge that is his,
And you'll go away enchanted
As my small garden is.

How Does Your Garden Grow?

The flowers I love the best of all
Are on my humble lawn.
They close their eyes with evening skies
And wake to greet the dawn.
    Daffodil looks quite like me,
    For-Get-Me-Not does, too,
    But tiny, toddling Lily White
    Looks, oh, so much like you.

But when a line of fairy frocks
Is hung out in the sun,
And all the flowers have changed their hues,
I'll still love every one,
    Love Daisy, who was Daffodil,
    For-Get-Me-Not, changed hue,
    And tiny, toddling Violet
    Who looks so much like you.

The Gallery

The color is here, and the passion. Yes.
It is a work that I can understand. I feel
The background, there. It burns me with its cold.
And yet the foreground,
With a small bird on a branch,
Has spoiled it all for me. Your bird is dead,
Wired to his perch, his feathers hunched in death.

Have you not seen
The character in birds? The tilted head,
Inquiring eye, the small breast bursting with
A curiosity that draws him, this most frail,
Most vulnerable of creatures, down to earth?
That is a bird.

No live bird paused for this, my friend.
Your bird is dead.
I see him, posed by careful hands, arranged,
Songless …. wingless,
Caught by fate and tamed
To be a model for your masterpiece.

My eyes are wet, and you can smile
At this, your utmost accolade. I wonder if
You cannot sense revulsion in my mind
Or if you did this by design, and I
Am seeing what you wanted me to see ...
A Spirit, crucified.

*****Inspired by a visit to the Crocker Museum,
Sacramento, California, 1966*****

Limitations

I was born to be an eagle of the crags,
With majesty in my slow circling,
With power I would swoop and glide and spin,
The world would turn upon my downward wing ...

Instead, the earth must orbit on its own.
I find I am earthbound in everything.
Through some mistake I walk within my cage,
A small, sad bird who cannot even sing.

*****Dedicated to Lurch, the Mynah bird - 1960's*****

Black Earth Love

Have you ever seen plowed black earth turning back
 Against the meadows green, an ebon track
 Leading to the sun and back again,
 Or clasping close a field of golden grain?
Oh, he who holds these fields close to his heart,
 Is of these fields, can solve life's mystery,
 For in black earth is found the hand of God,
 The hand of God, and more of poetry.

Have you ever seen the red earth, red as blood,
 Or crimson waters running sullen mud,
Red fingers twisting starving roots, no breeze,
A hundred scorching suns on shriveled leaves?
 Here hunger is … will be … has always been,
 And shanties grow from crying, dying earth
 Until their roofs slant over, tumble in,
And laughter lives in wild, abandoned mirth.

I must return ere black earth love has died,
Bounded by red land on every side,
To grow in corn, gold tasseled, waving high
And squares of wheat against an autumn sky.
My heart came forth from this black, plow-tamed land,
And shall return again a tall, tall tree,
For in black earth is found the hand of God,
The hand of God, and more of poetry.

A Garden

A garden isn't hard to make,
Flowers of every hue,
A painted bench beneath a tree,
Of Robin's egg blue,
A few tall blades of striped grass
That fairies hide under,
A twisted tree to wave its arms
And scare off thunder,
A few small dreams to dream about ...
And what else does it take?
A simple thing a garden is
And not hard to make.

October's Oklahoma

On Oklahoma evenings
When October's brush is laid
On every stunted jack oak
And elm tree in the glade,
When the sky is shot with color
From the sunset in the west
And the leaves are red and yellow,
I think that time is best.

The smell of roaring bonfires
Permeates the frosty breeze,
Like the glory of the sunset
And the glory of the trees.
I like to think of Indians …
Spirits dancing 'round the flame …
And feel a pride and glory in Oklahoma's name.

Then comes a sound of singing
As the sun sinks out of sight,
And the fragrant smoke wafts slowly
Through a chill October night.
Someone from out the darkness
Strums a song of Indian men.
On clear October evenings,
Oklahoma's pretty then.

*****This poem was inspired by two
happy Octobers spent in Byng, Oklahoma.
Published when Aola was 17 years old,
Golden Harvest, Mistletoe Press, 1937 *****

The Quiet Hour

There is a quiet hour when the sun
Has touched the evening sky with flaming rose
That lingers till the evening shadows run
In darkening lines across the west where glows
The last faint color of the day. The dun
Loam of the new-plowed field gives out
The rich warm fragrance of the earth, and one
Lone elm tree bends its head in a devout
And love reverence toward approaching night.

Somehow, dusk sifts down with gentle peace,
Veiling in tenderness each pointed height
That reaches to the sky, 'til stars release
Pale silvery chains of sapphire-jeweled light,
And small birds nod upon each leafy limb
And in a sleepy melody recite
With low crooned notes their little vesper hymn.

AGING

Aola, forever beautiful, 1977

One Dream

She was old when first I knew her.
She was old, and gray, and grim,
And her little, gray-walled cottage
Was as colorless and prim.
She was too old for laughter
And too reserved for tears,
So, she went primly down the path
Of gray, grim weary years
And never saw the daffodils
That grew beside the way,
Or paused to hear the blue bells chime
Or children at their play.
If she heard brushing fairy wings,
She grimly shook her head
And closed her ears to foolish things,
Went deaf and blind instead.

But when we heard that she was ill
And needed food and care,
We all took turns to help her …
Those brave enough to dare.
Oh, she would fret and fume at first,
But then her eyes grew dim,
And her gray, old face was softened,
And then she spoke of him.
He was coming, she said softly,
When the first flower saw the sun.
She'd waited fifty weary springs,
But she still knew he would come.
"He said that he'd come back to me
When he heard the first bird sing,
And that is why I cannot die.
I must see one more spring."

Today she lay in silence with
Spring's first flower at her throat,
And a bird outside the window sang
In golden, melting note.
She faced the last great stillness with
A smile, half calm, half merry,
And I was thankful for a Spring,
Spring come in January.

Understanding

I saw a house in a field of clover,
Grown too old and bending over.
I raised my palsied, twisted hand
To let it know I understand.
For we are worn by many years
And many fears,
And many tears.
I raise my hand.
I understand
When I see a house in a field of clover,
Grown too old and bending over.

Grow Old Gracefully

Old things have an inherent loveliness,
Such as old lace and weary, blue-veined hands,
And flowers pressed in Bibles, lullabies,
And silver hair and worn wide wedding bands.

Old things have such a grace and majesty,
So far removed from bitterness and strife,
And old ones fold their hands and smilingly,
In quietude, sit still and look at life.

Oh, God, I have been happy ... sorely tried ...
But let me feel that peace at eventide.

Still Those Tints Abide

I climbed up in a cherry tree,
So long ago, ago,
A tree that wore a rosy robe
Of sunset tinted snow.

But that was long ago, my dear,
And now the little tree
Is old and worn and twisted quite.
Yes, it is quite like me.

And sometimes, when the bright sun shines,
In all its warming glow,
I sometimes think it wishes for
Its robe of sunset snow.

And so I do. I sometimes, too,
But still those tints abide.
The cherry tree and I still wear
Our robe of dreams inside.

Cornstalk Fiddle

"My pretty little pink, I once did think
That you and I would marry ... "
Over the valley and through the hills
The dancing wild notes carry,
And o'er the meadows the pulsing beat
Of clapping hands and tapping feet,
A song of magic that thrills the trees
And sets them singing against the breeze.
The magic comes from beyond the hill,
Played to the tune of a Master's will
On a cornstalk fiddle, by an old, old man.

And then the music slows a beat
And clasping hands are parted.
Choose a couple in, choose a couple out
To cheer the broken hearted.
Through the valley the music sings,
A symphony of singing strings,
A crying, sighing sort of sound
That lies along the dewy ground,
That lifts on soaring wings to rise
And beat its wings against the skies.
Just a cornstalk fiddle and an old, old man.

Then comes the grayness that heralds dawn,
And the rest of the sun is stirred
By a last sweet note that reaches heights
Like the flight of a frightened bird.
A mournful note, a heartbreak note
That dies in the morning's golden throat
When the sun looks out with shining eyes
From his golden throne in the eastern skies,
To gild the gray of a bowed old head,
To touch a fiddle with music dead ...
Just a broken fiddle and a tired, old man.

Day's End

Weary I am. Too soon the setting sun
To see the tasks I rose to ever done,
Too late to miss the tired, sometimes tears.
Yet this day will illume my later years.

For when my hands grow old and idle, they
Will lift the draught of dreams I've brewed today.
With smiles and tears commingled will I sup.
Tonight, I am too tired to lift the cup.

Reverie in Rain

As a child I watched the rain
Drape silver plaits across the pane
Surrounding my small room, and I
Heard a soft, thrumming lullaby.

A feeling is the rain today.
Inscrutable and chill and gray ...
A reprimand from one I love,
A bony hand in moldy glove.

And so it is with moon and sun.
They light the best and worst of one;
The lines of years and care they trace
Caricaturing childhood's face.

I wish to find the friendly rain,
Illuminate ideals again,
Erase the years that made me wise,
Enchant the earth with childhood's eyes.

Or, if a tale is not twice told,
Find recompense in growing old.

Growing Weather

Love is like the crimson of the rose
With life the slender stem on which it grows.
With sun its perfect petals last unfold
To show its shining treasure … heart of gold.
We've found in golden lanes, tear-silvered trails,
The perfect love in growing old together.
True love blooms like the roses. Oh, my dear …
Our lives have known such lovely growing weather!

Spring Comes Out of January

She is older than the blossoms that she keeps
Pressed in a book of poems, ages old,
As frail as fragrant petals, dry as dust,
And clinging fast to fancies old ones hold.

She shows her faded flowers most reverently
To those who pass that way and chance to tarry.
"These are my sign that life comes out of death,
And spring comes ever out of January."

"Here is a crocus that I found
A singing April day
When I was but a small child,
And then again, in May,

"When I was grown a slim girl,
I found in grass dew wet,
Searching for a love note,
A fragrant violet,

"And this was once a red rose
I carried one bright June,
A silver trailing bride's bouquet
To Love's cascading tune,

"And once I wore a white rose
Upon a Mother's Day,
And this pale rose I found where
My child, last sleeping, lay.

"Oh, violets are Love's song,
And roses I remember …
But goldenrod showed me the sun
One chill and bleak November."

She clings close to the fancies old ones hold
And turns the faded pages, one by one,
And in these crumbling symbols of a life,
Is somehow caught and held the summer sun.

She shows her faded flowers most reverently
To those who pass that way and chance to tarry.
These are my sign that life comes out of death ...
And spring comes ever out of January.

The Little Hills

Somebody said there was gold in the little hills.
I followed the trail, and the stars, and the sunset's call.
Here at the long trail's end, where the whip-poor-wills
Are singing their lonely hymns, I have found it all.

Here where the silences are, have I bent to till,
Where the hills weep shadows of amethyst and of gray,
For here there are stones, and silences and soil,
And here have I molded monuments in clay.

My hands are hard with the work they have learned to do.
My eyes are keen with a dream, and a seeking to find,
But my hands have learned to be soft and gentle, too,
And my eyes look to the hills, for the hills are kind.

Tonight, I am old, and again the whip-poor-wills
Lure me to far horizons to seek a new dream's call.
Sunsets and stars build dreams in the little hills.
For me there is no more gold. I have found it all.

Sunbonnet Sue

Sunbonnet Sue in a gingham dress,
Perched on the top of an old rail fence,
Long braids feeling the wind's caress,
Just six years old now, and would you guess …
Queen of the prairies so immense.

Sunbonnet Sue, in her muslins fine,
Hooped and laced and prim and staid,
Grown up to the age of six and nine,
But her prim mouth's sweet, and her shy eyes shine
With the grace of a prairie maid.

Sunbonnet Sue in her calico,
Washed and faded, tired and worn …
A few more hours 'til the sun must go
And her basket is filled to overflow,
Filled with garments tiny and torn.

Sunbonnet Sue at the close of day,
Gown of silk and folded hands,
Her hair is frosted a silver gray,
But her eyes are young, and they survey
The slow sun sinking upon her lands.
Sunbonnet Sue, it is time for rest,

And the sun is lost from view,
Save a crimson shaft that streaks the West
To touch locks many suns caressed.
The West belongs to you, Sunbonnet Sue.

This Is My Sign

As Winter coldly clasped my red bud tree,
It came to me
That I was growing old. I longed to cling
To Autumn's gold, see sharp stars swing
Against the season's urge, and know that Spring
Was certainty ...
As Winter coldly clasped my red bud tree.

But then I thought how many years I'd seen
The grass grow green,
And long black furrows turning from the plow
From sun to sun. I can see now
The tinge of mauve along the red bud's bough
In glowing sheen.
This is my sign. I shall not cease to dream.

PASSING

Bill
June 7, 1920 – January 9, 2002

Aola
May 7, 1920 – February 21, 1989

If I Should Go

If I should go before the Evensong,
To cross alone the silent sea,
Remember this, some temples stand too long,
And do not cry for me.

And as I stand before the golden throne
Then I shall kneel and ask a word,
That He may comfort those I've left alone.
This I shall pray, my Lord.

If I should go before the Evensong,
Then lift your eyes and look above.
Do not let sorrow's shadow come between
To hide my prayer, my love.

For we both know there is no final knell
To end the memories that are.
Close your ear against the sounding bell.
Instead, seek out a star.

The Shadowed Stair

Across the shadowed room your eyes are kind,
And filled with dreams that I have known. I, too,
Have felt the breathless hush of twilight hour,
A quiet call that comes to me ... to you.

And if you choose to answer, slip away,
As quietly as night slips into day,
Then I shall hold the peace that we have loved
Nor lift a hand nor lift my voice to stay.

And after, when a twilight comes again,
And a night wind gently rocks your empty chair,
Then I shall raise my eyes as I do now,
And see you sitting, rocking, smiling there.

And when you turn to point the shadowed stair,
I shall with sure, swift hands turn down the light,
And moving to you, take your gentle hand
To wait the rest and peacefulness of night.

Insight

Now I see why those who dream
Love life no more than death,
For life is measured not by time
And shortened with each breath,
But life is fuller after life,
And this the dreamers know.
They take life's beauty in their arms
And hold it closer so.

Ebbtide

I shall take my tired soul
And body to the sea.
The waves that dream along the shore
Will comfort me,
Will comfort me.

I shall lie still upon the sands,
Know sorrow not, nor happy be,
But in a drowsy languor lie
In apathy,
In apathy.

The waves will fold their arms in warm
Serenity about me there.
A golden net in soft green depths
Will be my hair,
Will be my hair.

The waves will ebb. The waves will ebb,
And leave me on my coral isle,
And I shall wear, in soft dim sleep,
A secret smile,
A secret smile.

Now in November

An old book of poems and an open fire,
Fires flame, frosts chill hate and desire.
Gold trees and crimson ones running down a hill,
Winds like a love song … winds bitter chill.
Red cheeks and gay eyes, smiling, free and bold.
Blue lips and wan face, hiding from the cold.
Smoke rising like a spire … smoke slowly shifting,
Down on a new grave, leaves gently drifting.

To Question Why

There are so many, many things
That we shall never know,
How death can chain an eagle's wings,
And winters turn to fragrant springs,
And where the dead dreams go.

But is it wrong to wonder, wrong
To question, question why?
Why must a blue bird cease his song,
Why is infinity so long,
Why must all loved things die?

I questioned all with downcast eyes
For what are all these things?
I heard no sound, but in the skies,
I saw the clouds bow down and rise
To a shadow as of wings.

Where I Shall Lie

This is the place where I shall lie
When the stars go out in the winter sky.
Here I shall be with friends, and here
The ones I've loved will all be near.
Here I shall dream my dreams and rest
As a far-off sun sinks in the West.

Here I shall learn the way of peace …
Of silences that do not cease.
Here I'll remember lovely things,
And hear the whispering of wings
'Til the sun comes up in the eastern sky …
This is the place where I shall lie.

Pastel Fairies

When I was just a little girl
I had a small white bed
With pastel fairies painted
On the posts at foot and head.
The fairies all would bow their heads
At night my prayers to hear
And wake me at the dawning with
"It's morning time, mos' dear."

But now I'm not a little girl
The bed's gone long ago.
The pastel fairies flew away
As someday I must go.
I sometimes wish when last I wake,
Wish that last dawn to hear
The pastel fairies softly say,
"It's morning time, mos' dear."

*****Aola Seery, published at age 17,
Golden Harvest, Mistletoe Press, 1937*****

Fear

You shall walk singing through the shadows,
For you are brave ... so brave,
And there is but a little way
'Twixt Heaven and the grave.
You shall walk singing ... singing,
With faith and not a fear,
Through the vale of no returning
For you are like that, dear.

Yet you have not seen blood and war
And hate in eyes of men
And death in all its dreariness ...
Would you go singing then?
Yes, Heaven is so near, I know,
And I believe this thing,
But I fear that before I go,
I shall forget to sing.

The Song of the Pinewood Tree

She was as wild as an elfin child.
Her spirit was that of the sea,
And the song she sang 'til the wooded hills rang
Was the song of the pinewood tree.

She was as gay as a summer day,
And her flight was swift as the swallow
Where the mists spill silver on the hill
And the violets hide in the hollow.

She was as free as the stormy sea,
And her soul was the wings of the morning …
'Til the deepening snow made her feet grow slow …
And she left them, sympathy scorning.

She lay as still as the stones on the hill,
Where we laid her to rest … but after
The song of the sea and the pinewood tree
Was the sound of familiar laughter.

Not the Way of You

Last night I dreamed that you were dead,
But that cannot be true,
For somehow death, as I have said,
Seems not the way of you.

And if it is, and you are dead,
Your life was not complete.
Too bitter was the brew you drank
At times, and then too sweet.

Your spirit, if my dream was true
Will, from Death's reposes,
Send bursts of leaves and shredding thorns
Reaching up to roses.

I shall not weep that you are dead,
For I may come ever
To touch each rose above your head …
You, who loved me never.

Oh, somehow death, as I have said,
Seems not the way of you,
A rose is withered in my hand.
I wonder where it grew.

Nine Pins

Child crossing the road at the eve of the day,
A car like a demon roars out of the grey.
Can't stop, takes a life, and screams on its way.

And deep in the earth, deep down in his den
Old Satan is playing at nine pins again.

Get out of the way he's ready to bowl,
An auto his ball and a human his goal …
And be not the driver who helps him take toll.

When deep in the earth, deep down in his den
Old Satan is playing at nine pins again.

***** Aola Seery, published at age 17,
Golden Harvest, Mistletoe Press, 1937*****

Where Shamrocks Grow

Don't be after cryin', Michael lad,
Or thinkin' that I'm goin' far away …
For I'm goin' with your two strong arms about …
And hearin' words I've loved to hear you say.
And I am seein' Death, now, Michael lad.
Death is an isle … an isle that we two know …
An isle of emerald lakes. Dear, don't be sad.
My feet are deep in grass where shamrocks grow.

I've seen the sea bring bodies to the shore,
And women standin' keenin' by the wave.
They think that life begins, and life must end …
A spirit can be prisoned in a grave.
Go tell them, tell them for me, Michael lad,
Life's sea has cast me on a shore I know.
That death is but a dream, a dream fulfilled.
My feet are deep in grass where shamrocks grow.

Fools

I knew that he was Death, but I went to the door,
And asked him in.
We chatted awhile, over our teacups.
The war in China, we discussed, and sit-down strikes,
And scientific farming, and then he rose and yawned.
"Why not come along?"
"Which route are you taking?"
"I think I shall go through the Valley of Darkness.
The road is a trifle rough, but there are signs along the way.
I shall enjoy your company."
"Not yet, Old Fool," I laughed. "I'm much too young.
I've other roads to travel yet and many things to see."
"I swear," he said, "I like your spirit!
In half a life, by old time's clock, I'll come again,
And we shall see
Who is the Fool!"

———

Prisoner

In my bunk inside the cell
When night's shade falls on the room,
I think of many things and watch
The iron bars march 'cross the moon.
And high in the sky with unwinking eye
A star with the dawn calls down a goodbye.

And when death comes to call me home
To heaven or hades whiche'er my goal,
When they gaze upon my heart, they'll see
The iron bars march 'cross my soul.
And high in the sky with unwinking eye
The star will have heard my last goodbye.

***** Aola Seery, published at age 17,
Golden Harvest, Mistletoe Press, 1937*****

Don't Be Afraid

When we were little kids enough
To think that we were big
And whittle willow whistles
From a little willow twig
And imitate the bird's call,
I'd leap across the blue
And running waters of the brook
And reach my arms to you.

"Come on," I'd say, "Don't be afraid,
'Cause I won't let you fall …"
And you would shut your eyes and jump,
And not be scared at all.

Then, when we grew a little more,
I had to go away.
Before I went, I asked you
To wait and name the day,
And when you hesitated
To answer yes, your sighs
Were ended as I took your hand
And looked into your eyes.

"Come on," I said, "Don't be afraid,
And marry me this fall."
You shut your eyes and answered yes …
And weren't scared at all.

But now, today, you lie so still
I know a nameless fear …
Can only sit beside you
And try to hold you here.
There is a gulf between us …
There's nothing I can do
But stand upon the shore this side
And reach my arms to you.

"Come on, my dear … don't be afraid …
'Cause I won't let you fall.
Just shut your eyes and come to me …
And don't be scared at all."

Hospital Waiting Room

Unquiet walls, mid white robed figures noiseless tread,
You've stood in spotless purity these many years,
Cleansed by faith and love and silver tears,
To bound this place of living sorrow … silent dead.
White robed figures noiseless tread … unquiet walls,
The ghosts of dreams and courage tread these halls,
A proof that all things live and all things last …
And I who lived my life in my poor way
And counted time and life from day to day
Am crowded by these visions from the past.

Unquiet walls that stare dispassionately,
And lights that glare and glimmer and grow dim …
I sit and watch, unbreathing, and I see
A thousand dreams forgotten, moving in
Bounded by these blank, unquiet walls,
Dark huddled watchers wait with bated breath.
White robed figures tread the chill broad halls,
And speak the words put on their lips by Death.

Death Is Like a Paneled Door

Death is like a paneled door ...
A paneled door, and it is closed so tightly,
And I, I only hold the key.
And so it is, and still, I hear you nightly,
Faltering footsteps, calling, calling me ...
A paneled door, so frail, so frail between,
A slender barrier twixt life and death.
Somewhere, somewhere, a hush'ed wind goes crying,
And mingled in it, ghost of your life's breath ...
And still your soul is weeping at the windows.
A paneled door is this, and yet, so thin ...
I know my life, when slow at last I answer,
Will be smothered by your great soul rushing in.

To Fifty Years

Ah, it's fare-thee-well to fifty years and a fond hello to now,
There's a waiting ship with silver sails and a gay, sun-golden prow.
There's a dusty road that leads to Spain and blowing Scottish heather,
And she and I walk side by side, a-swinging hands together.
We wander, as we've always wished, paths we have never trod,
And I am seen, and she unseen ... half-way 'twixt me and God.

And we're laughing, ever laughing, as we go from place to place,
And dark-skinned people wonder at the laughter in my face.
They cannot see as I can see, as I look toward the skies,
The dancing laughter answer in her sweet, beguiling eyes.
They cannot hear, as I can hear, as I list to the hills,
The music of her laughter in a thousand silver rills.

And I have heard the music of her bare, brown dancing feet,
Have heard her husky whisper in an old Italian street,
Have heard her silver singing in a multitude of things,
And found a certain music in the hushing sound of wings,
And, oh, we weave a web of dreams about the things we see,
And I am seen, and she unseen, half-way 'twixt God, and me.

*****Aola Seery, published at age 17,
Golden Harvest, Mistletoe Press, 1937*****

Soul-Strings

When that part of mine earthly self which feels
The pain and sorrowing in all things here,
When that one part, that tight strung trembling lute
On which the crashing chords of life are roughly struck
Has snapped beneath the fingers of this world
And sent its last notes trembling to the skies,
I shall have found the solace I have sought.
I shall have reached the pinnacle of peace.

But now I sit and now I sigh, for all
My thoughts sit 'round and watch, and their sick stare
Has put a madness and a fever in my brain,
A flame which burns eternal, and I long
For cool dark places and the endless space
Which I shall know when I have quenched my thirst
With cup of death and gone unto my rest.

When my last chord has sounded, and
When my last song is sung,
I'll thank God with my one last breath
Lutes cannot be restrung.

You Grieve - I Sing

I know it must seem strange that I should sing
Here on my knees beside a grassy mound …
No hymn, no lullaby, no sorrow's sound …
A song she used to love, a fairy thing,
A song of dusk and stars and how they bring
A silver cup of dew-wine to the ground,
Drop little wishes where they may be found
When it is May, and May has brought the spring.
But I have searched for wishes through the grass
And found but thorns that pierced my fingers deep,
But I shall sing it for my little lass …
I know she would be sad to see me weep.
Along the grassy paths the people pass
I kneel and sing, though she is fast asleep.

Folded Wings

I think that Death must come on splendid wings
To those who follow suns across the skies,
And dreams of Heaven's glory bright he brings
To hold a time, at peace, the seeking eyes,
Fulfillment of their dreams … these shall arise.
A lullaby of triumph thus he sings.
These shall hold rein of lightning through the skies.
I think that Death must come on splendid wings.

And then, again, Death wears a sable cloak,
And comes through twilit lanes on quiet feet,
Where nothing breathes, and in the silence smoke
Lies somnolent on hills where peace is sweet.
Death walks at dusk a quiet, sleepy street
To find a weary face among the folk,
To lull one to a kind, unbreathing sleep.

Spiritual Rest

I left my heart upon a hill
When spring walked on the sod,
And the air was sweet with Clover blooms,
And a stallion newly shod
Left hoof prints on the mossy turf
As he paused upon the brink
Of the spring with laughter brimming full,
And bent his head to drink.

I left my heart upon a hill
Of heartaches none have I.
I left it where the dawn first walks,
Where the green hill meets the sky,
Where the Meadow lark nests in the grass,
I left my heart until
Someday perchance I go to rest
With my heart upon the hill.

*****Aola Seery, published at age 17,
Golden Harvest, Mistletoe Press, 1937*****

Derelict

Eyeless you stand, with hollow stare of death
In eyes that in their last long sleep do only dream
Of time when time was young and life and breath
Were pulsing in thy body, and a gleam
Was in thine eyes. All this white sifted dust
That lies in robes of death about thy feet
In sullen silence … ashes in the dusk …
Is but a winding sheet.

Singing in the Sun

She doesn't sleep, for somewhere she doth run,
Light-hearted, free, and singing in the sun.
So little time she had for singing here,
Or running where the brook runs swift and clear,
For time took youth and song, and even breath ...
I think she must have smiled when she saw Death.
I think she must have smiled her gentle smile,
And gone to meet Him on that last dim mile,
And when He had released her pinioned wings,
Soared upward ... on to brighter, lovelier things ...
And left her weariness, her sorrow, and her pain
To turn again to that from whence they came ...

But you, within your little worlds, your spheres,
Attempt to weight her feet with mortal tears,
And still, you feel a sorrow, know a pain
Though suns have set and risen ... set again.
Oh, do not weep for she is with you still ...
She's singing in an ecstasy atop a sunlit hill!
She's singing in an ecstasy ... a caged bird been set free!
She's laughing in a silver stream that runs down to the sea ...
A sea so very wide and deep ... a sea so very blue ...
A sea so very like the love that she still bears for you!
She lived her life ... and lived it well, and now that it is done,
She's watching for your coming and singing in the sun.
You'll go to her along the way her Angel feet have trod.
Some call it death, some call it sleep, but I ...
I call it God.

FAITH

Aola,
Photo sent to Bill in England, WWII

Bill,
Photo sent to Aola from England, WWII

Belief

The green corn grew in sun and rain
   Lifting between the foolish clods
   Raising its tasseled head to gain,
   Aid from the elements, its gods,

But a few lone stocks believe'd not
   And bowing said there is no God.
   Should we to strive in barren spot?
   Strive and die, return to sod?

The green stalks sighed, compassion filled
   And sent a rustling breeze to tell,
   That they might live, they who so willed
   To cast the name of infidel.

Raise high thy shaft into the morn,
   Press down thy roots into the loam,
   That your soul may the heap adorn
   When Jesus takes the harvest home.

***** Aola Seery, published at age 17,
Golden Harvest, Mistletoe Press, 1937*****

Home at Twilight

I pray to Thee that I may be
A person of simplicity,
And through the storm, past evil's wraith,
Hold high the lantern of my faith,
And though I roam and walk alone,
May twilight bring this sinner home.

And this I pray, that day to day,
I may lead others on the way,
The way to right, though dark the night,
To meet my God in blazing light,
And he will come in evening gloam,
Through shadowed paths to lead me home.

And grant me this … I may not miss
The warm rain's tears, the soft wind's kiss,
And laughter, love, and sorrow's sigh,
Let me live fully, let me die,
And though I roam and walk alone,
May twilight bring this sinner home.

Resurrection

A faint white morning deepens,
Its veils of mist unfold
And lie along the far-off hills
In crimson and in gold.
From out my shining window
I see the dawning day,
And kneel beside with folded hands
And bended knee to pray.

Father, somehow on this day
The world seems born anew.
Across the hills and through the gray
The new day comes in view.
Across the stirring spring-filled hills
A promise sweet is said
Of rising from the depths of deeps
As one rose from the dead.

And then across the hills there comes
A sound of chimes and song;
A whisper chant that swells to sound
Of deep-toned notes, and long,
And as my new-born soul looks up
To where he leads the way,
My heart looks out with prayerful eyes
To greet the newborn day.

Prayer Perfect

Oh, perfect day with glory in its ending,
With quiet, wind-whirled clouds that brush the moon,
With purple shadows into gold wheat blending,
With sweet, small roses redolent of June.

Oh, perfect night, on swift, still wings approaching …
Oh, perfect dream that treads its starlit way …
Oh, perfect hour of sweet anticipation,
Wherein I kneel in prayer …
Oh, perfect day!

The Fisherman

When the lamp of courage fails, and shadow things
Invade the mind, despoil the heart and soul,
And man has tried, and bruised his reaching wings
And searches for a way to become whole.
When clouds are heavy cushions on his eyes
And suns become too torrid long to bear,
Then he should leave his burden where it lies
And search for healing in the Anywhere.
A man should have the sunlight on the sea,
A long horizon lie to search and know,
Should cast a line for lesser things than he
And feel his strength return and surge and flow.
His wars with man and time, his lonely fight
Will cease, for in vast stillness God is there,
And he will see things in their proper light
And find his healing in the Anywhere.

For Jesus

I would be eyes for Jesus,
But yet I shrink to see
The bloody ways of war-torn worlds,
The sin surrounding me.

I would be ears for Jesus,
But, oh, a cry of fear ….
Hushed whispers in a house of death,
Are dreadful things to hear.

I would be hands for Jesus,
But building temples tall
Is not a thing that I can do.
They'd topple, and they'd fall.

No, I am not brave, nor strong,
I hear no sound of wings
For Jesus somehow did not mean
For me to do these things.

But while I have a single crust,
No one shall hungry go …
The little things, the beaten things,
I'll help to stand and grow.

And while I cannot be his eyes,
Nor ears, nor hands apart …
With meekness and with mercy, I
Shall strive to be his heart.

High Noon

Golden noon, sun shining high,
And blanketed in sorrow yet I lay,
Blinded by the blueness of the sky,
Hoping, steeped in slumber,
To dream my grief away.

The air was sweet with smell of fresh turned sod
Of fields, long furrows stretching to the sun.
The bees were drowsy with the sun, and God
Shook blossoms down upon my face
From off the plum.

The droning bees and shimmering heat brought peace.
The turbulence of outer worlds grew dead.
So, I arose and went a lighter way,
The glory of noon sun
In my head.

***** Aola Seery, published at age 17,
Golden Harvest, Mistletoe Press, 1937*****

Man of Galilee

"Suffer little children to come unto me ... "
So said the Man of Galilee,
And that is the reason that I know
How a ragged child in the winter snow
And the chilling wind of the frozen mart
Could give me a smile that warmed my heart ...
And that is why the lame lad walked,
And that is why the dumb child talked,
And I saw a blind boy's look of awe,
And I've often wondered what he saw,
And a deaf boy told me that he'd heard
A splendid song, a whispered word ...
And that is the reason, when I pray,
My years of sorrow fall away,
And I, a small child, come to Thee
To worship, Man of Galilee.

———————

Country Church

A hymn, the organ of their voices,
Echoes in the quiet place.
Transfiguration ... quiet glory
In the stillness of each face ...
Glory lost but on the baby.
Ah, how sweet, so sweet he slumbers,
Time is but an hour for laughter.
Clocks are playthings with queer numbers.
Time is meant for old and infirm,
Clocks for him when he grows older.

Now he's sleeping, flushed and rosy,
Slumbering on Mummy's shoulder.
See big sister, blushing, conscious
Of bold glance of luckless swains,
Thinking of her chosen escort,
Going home through country lanes.
Ring on white and slender finger,
First time bared to sight of all.
Small, effective mute announcement
Of the wedding in the fall.

Side by side sit Mums and Daddy,
Next to Grandma, old and wise,
Holy light of many ages
Glows in Mother's tired eyes.
She has in her eyes a glory.
Visions holy in her sight,
Pain and tears and such forgotten ...
Haloed head in holy light.
Lighted candles in their holders
On her shed their bright caress.

Daddy's proud to sit beside her …
Angel in a faded dress.
Time to go. The pastor closes
Holy Book. The people rise
And get their wraps, and little brother
Wakens, opens drowsy eyes.
Children all wrapped up in blankets,
Tucked securely in the sleigh,
Laughing merrily, start homeward,
Singing softly half the way.

Soon the children hush … near sleeping,
And across the snow, blue white,
Daddy guides the plunging horses,
God walks with them through the night.
Then home, and Mums, while Dad unhitches,
Heats milk to drink … cuts gingerbread.
The children all bring down their blankets,
By the heat stove make their bed.
Mums and Daddy bring more blankets
Cover well their sons and heirs.

Heated bricks and silently, a-tip-toe,
Steal off to cold and bleak upstairs.
Then Sister comes. She warms her fingers,
Slips upstairs, just like a mouse.
The Great God smiles and draws sleep's curtain
All around the little house.
Plain people these … of earth and plodding,
Yet they have felt a joy sublime,
And I have seen each face transfigured
In the church … at Meeting time!

The Gift of Flowers

A dusty little gutter-pup
Found a yellow buttercup
Blowing by the side of a dismal city street,
Growing in a crack of a narrow, dingy street.
He sniffed its perfumed fragrance up,
Then took the yellow buttercup
And laid the golden flower at a ragamuffin's feet,
Laid the wilted blossom at his little master's feet.

If we could bring a little sun
Into the heart of such a one …
A smile bring, like a flower, unto everyone we meet,
Give a gift of laughter unto everyone we meet,
Then we would find that there was none
Of shadow for us, only sun …
Because our Master found our gift, our gift of flowers sweet,
Because our Master found our gift, our gift was very sweet.

Little Boy Lost

"Mother, who made God?" he asked,
And I, who did not know,
Yet knew I must support his faith,
I gave my answer so …

"I do not know," I said,
But the childish faith of his
Looked out from disappointed eyes,
And then I said, "He is."

"He is the sky behind the clouds,
The clouds before the sky.
He is where bluebells sway and chime …
In every butterfly."

"He is the shining of the sun,
The singing in the streams.
He is the rock that stands the storm,
The loveliness of dreams."

"Mother, who made God?" he asked.
Now, with my earthly woes,
I find a solace in the thought
That now … somewhere, he knows.

The blue skies smile with all the stars,
At that childish faith of his,
An echo lost in pain comes back …
"He is … He is … He is!"

Pioneers

God gave them vision and the power to dream.
They saw a beauty in a raw, red, rugged land.
They made a slave of every shallow stream
That struggled o'er the stone and clay and sand.
God gave them strength and power to endure
For the way was new. The trail was wild and hard.
God went ahead and broke and blazed the trail.
When sentries slept, He took his turn at guard.

God gave us vision and the power to dream.
We have no worlds to conquer, no new trail,
Yet we must cross our mountains, follow gleam.
He guards us lest we cease our quest and fail.
He helps us make a slave of every thought
And make of it a good, known far and wide.
How can we fail, though rude and crude, untaught,
With love and truth and faith and God to guide.

****Aola Seery, published at age 17,
Golden Harvest, Mistletoe Press, 1937****

The Message

"Go unto all the world," He said, but she
Was born to never walk and could not see,
And all the shadows of her darkening gloom
Were bound into the four walls of a room.
"Go unto all the world." Her only prayer
Was that her Lord might hear her … hear her there,
And let her talk to ears that had not heard
The precious message of His glorious word.

I wonder if she knew, when last He came
To take her by the hand to speak her name,
How well that she had spread his message there
Where she sat beside the window in her chair,
With splendid faith in eyes that did not see,
And in her twisted self such majesty.
And I who passed the window saw these things
And heard the whispering sound of angel wings.

Crucifixion

An old rugged cross	A pain twisted figure
Stands on a hill.	Next to the skies …
On it my Savior	Sorrow of ages
Is crucified still.	Shadowing eyes.
My sins are the cruel nails,	I pray, Man of Sorrow,
The thorns in His crown …	That what I may do
Only my love can	Will not tomorrow crucify you.
Help Him down.	

The Touch of His Hand

The lights dimmed in the church and then went out,
The lightning only playing on the faces
Of the people as they sat in silence, awed.
They did not speak a word or leave their places,
For there was something there among us in the dark,
A something that came in on sandaled feet,
And someone sang a silver thread of song,
And, oh, the song was sweet, the song was sweet.

I fixed my gaze upon the candle flame
That bowed before the sound of brushing wings
And reached my hand to touch a white robe's hem
That came between my eyes and other things.
I raised my glance, and looking past His hands,
The wounded hands no doubter could disguise,
I gazed into the depths, the tenderness,
The asking and the knowing of His eyes.

The lights dimmed in the church. A moment there
I hid my eyes against His bleeding hand.
I saw a cross upon a rocky hill.
There was no growing thing in all that land.
Then back into the storm He went. I found
The blind eyes He had touched were wet with rain,
But there was much to see when, one by one,
The lights in all the church came on again.

―――――――

Prayer

Close my eyes to sorrow,
Close my eyes to tears.
Close my eyes to sadness …
Hasten these last years.

If I see much more weeping,
Many more chill skies,
I may forget the sunshine.
Father, close my eyes.

Close my ears to sighing.
Close my ears to pain.
Close my ears to warring.
Ease my troubled brain.

Close my ears to tumult.
Hasten these last years.
I may forget sweet music.
Father, close my ears.

Father, guide me homeward,
Lest I stumble … fall.
Let my eyes see but your face …
My ears hear but your call.

My footsteps ever follow
As you beckon to me, "Come,"
My footsteps never falter.
Father, guide me home.

Glory

Hearken all the children to the prophecy that God
Has set the wind, the singing wind to tell.
It sets the reeds to thrilling, the willow trees to sighing,
As it echoes o'er bleak hill and fertile dell.

There'll be glory in the morning.
Bless thy children, Lord!
And your sins will be forgiven.
Praise be!
There'll be glory in the morning,
And we'll hear His blessed word.
He will ope the gates of heaven
For thee.

There'll be glory in the morning.
Glory be to God!
You will gaze upon the pearly gates
And then?
There'll be glory in the morning
When you rise from out the sod,
Parted from thy sins.
Amen!

Hearken all ye children to the prophecy of God.
And ye who stopped and faltered, who have sinned,
Will find the peace you've needed and be clean for evermore
If you listen to the sighing of the wind.

*****Aola Seery, published at age 17,
Golden Harvest, Mistletoe Press, 1937*****

Man-Made

A man can make a man of wood,
Of marble, clay or lead,
Can shape a laughter on his lips,
Can shape a noble head.
A man can make a man to stand
Firm, straight and sound of limb.
A man can make a man, but who
Can put the God in him?

A man may make his happiness,
A man may make his sorrow,
But life in him he cannot make,
And life he cannot borrow.
A man may make a man of wood,
Of marble, clay or lead,
But none can put God in his heart,
Or God within his head.

Peace

How can I tell you, my brother,
The comforting peace that is prayer,
When all that you know is about you,
The darkness and storm that is there?
How can I show you the distance
That lies between glory and shame,
The time-measured life that is sorrow,
The infinite life in His name?

How can I lead you in pathways,
In paths where your feet should be led?
How can I lighten your burden
That you may be comforted?
How can I show you His pity
That reaches o'er land and o'er sea,
And bridges unbridgeable chasms
For feet of a sinner like me?

Look to the hills of His making ...
The greatest, the tiniest things ...
The clouds that are soft on the heavens,
The flash of a bluebird's wings,
The great dim hush of the twilight,
The great white flash of the day ...
Look to the hills of His making,
Then kneel, finite creature, to pray.

But you will not find Him, my brother,
Always in the things far above ...
Around you, beside you, and in you,
He speaks in the things that you love.
Search for Him, find Him, my brother.
Replenish your faith at His light.
Then hold it high up ... like a candle
To guide someone else through the night.

Not for This

It is not for this I'm thanking Thee,
The beauty of each leaf and flower and tree,
Placid lengths of hills against the kiss
Of dawn and evening suns. No, not for this.

This I thank Thee for, that I can see
In each and all these things the hand of Thee,
See Thy hand in symmetry of leaves,
Shade tapestries the sun through treetops weaves.

I've learned each flower's petal-rays to part,
And seeking, find Thee in each golden heart.
Leaning on a tree's rough bark my cheek,
I find the tender solace that I seek.

When each day begins, when each is done,
I look unto the hills from sun to sun.
'Tis for this that I am thanking Thee,
That Thou hast given all this unto me,

And though I see beauty, all apart,
I find deeper beauty in my heart.

I Found Peace

I found peace
In the sob of cooing doves
Breathed to the night,
In the drip of heaven born dew
On thirsty leaves,
In the depths of shadow-haunted lakes,
The slant of silver rain
Against the eaves
And old gray ivied walls of
Crumbling stone,
In needled paths throughout the forest dim,
And the strange earth smell of moss
In a wooded place
In a shrine where once I knelt
To pray to Him.

**** Aola Seery, published at age 17,
Golden Harvest, Mistletoe Press, 1937****

Judgment Day

The trumpet had sounded, and the earth stood still,
Dim in a maze of long blue light
That turned into shadows in life's long lanes,
And stopped in its starting the wild bird's flight.
The pulsing of the world stopped.
One black feather fell.
One single leaf dropped.
Once tolled a church bell.
My soul slid softly through a shade-filled sky,
Smaller than an atom, but greater than the moon
That sobbed in space with knowledge it must die,
And I cradled it to sleep and hummed a tune.

Stars shot down the dark,
Ten million in a breath,
Each one a mere spark,
An omen of death.
Thunder rolled across the skies in a mighty swell.
Lightning flashed on the riven tomb.
The whole haze flickered with the flames of Hell,
And little lost souls went winging through the gloom.
Eerie were the wind's sighs.
Weird was the wind's wail.
Light crackled down skies
In a comet's trail.

Stars flashing down skies told of deaths to be ...
Myriad, and small stars, but still I knew
When a small star fell, 'twas the life of me
That fell and was lost in the maze of blue.
Then all the skies whirled.
Down a million stars hurled.
Down went the dead world
To infinity,
All in a mad race,
Drawn to the central place
Which is God
And eternity.

My Prayer

Looking up at me with trusting eyes,
From where you kneel to say your little prayer,
You ask the question that I sigh to hear,
"Mother, who is God, and what and where?"

Who is God, and what is He, and where?
How can I tell him, "Son, I do not know,
For I have seen God only through your eyes,
In your being as I've watched you grow."

Once you were ill, and I, there waiting,
With futile fingers holding death away …
I, who had before known only hating,
How I wished that I had learned to pray.

Once when I watched you at your playing,
And saw your limbs were straight and strong and clean,
Then it was I came almost to praying,
But then there was a shadow in between.

I knew this day would come. It had to come,
When you would kneel at this time we have shared,
And half-asleep, and trusting, ask of God.
How to answer now … I'm so unprepared?

And as I draw my small boy to my knee,
Dear God, help me to say the things I should,
For here, and in my hands is this small soul,
Who am I to tell him what is good?

Help me to say the things a mother should,
Oh, dear Lord … dear God! What am I saying?
I, I who have not seen Thee face to face …
I see Thee now as I kneel here praying.

Salvation

I saw him there, so twisted and so bent,
Made pale and hunched and horrible by pain,

And there I paused and cursed, yea, cursed my God,
And looked into that shadowed face again.
"How can there be a God," so my thoughts ran,
"Unless he is some evil, scheming beast
Who lets stark pain dwell on when else has ceased,
And makes a harsh-faced horror of a man?"

For all the pain of mankind through the years,
I cursed my God, I did, and shed my tears.

He raised blank eyes of shadowed emptiness,
Where pain had killed expression in its youth.
His voice came stumbling through his teeth, and yet
I seemed to hear the ring of life and truth.
He showed me then the letters that he wrote
With dull, dead hands, he did, and each address
Was that of someone sick with loneliness,
A shut-in, or one void of faith and hope.

"I try," he said, "to ease their load of care…
For I have faith and love enough to share."

Ashamed, I left and went upon my way,
For faith so great before I had not seen,
So far removed from little, petty things,
The things that are so common and so mean.
'Twas then I knew he had been put on earth
To teach us all how blessed is our lot,
To give to us the faith that we have not,
And teach to us salvation … true faith's worth.

I lowered thankful eyes unto the sod …
For he had given back to me my God.

****Written at the age of 17.****

―――――――

God's World

Your mouth was hard and bitter
As you opened it to say
"Cold day." And I answered,
"Lovely day!"
And quietly, inside me,
In a wee voice all apart,
Came two small words, "God's Day!"
In my heart.

Your mouth was hard and bitter,
As you spoke about the rain,
Spoke in words of sorrow
And of pain.
"This will make the flowers bloom,"
I said. The small voice cried
These two small words, "God's gift!"
Deep inside.

Your mouth was hard and bitter,
And your lips with scorn were curled.
You went your way scoffing
At the world,
And quietly, and smiling,
I went with lighter tread.
"This is God's world, your world ..."
My voice said.

The Return

It did not seem that you would go away …
No more than hills we have been looking to.
The hills seemed less of strength to us than you,
And that is why it seemed that you would stay.
We hardly knew that you had gone that day,
But only after days did it seem true …
The joy we know now that you've come anew
Can't be expressed in words we know to say.

But maybe you can read it in our eyes
As we lay at your feet the goals we've won …
With, "here is a hurt heart to heal, Most Wise."
"Here is the newest dream I've dreamed," says one …
Our need of you is one that never dies.
We welcome you, now that your journey's done.

———

Foundations

God gave men talents and said, "Use them well."
He gave the earth, the sky, the elements.
Man found the good fruits and the bad thereof,
Made martial music, sweet songs, and laments.

And of the earth, he built small temples there,
Baked clay and straw and faith and sweat of brow,
Went on to build his tower of Babylon.
Where is that tower now?

God gave a man a mind and two strong hands,
A home, a hearth, a book of rules to follow,
Instructions not to build upon the sands,
But man looked up in envy of the swallow.

And of the earth, he made a golden calf,
He fashioned him a sword, a shield, a plow,
A ship, a plane, a bomb with God's own wrath.
Where is that power now?

Sometimes at night I watch great squadrons fanned
Against the sky. I see a house on sand
And know that sometime, somewhere we all must
Come to the final ashes and the dust.

For without God's love for its foundation
How can this age mean progress for our nation?

———

The Great Master

The master played on his violin.
His composition was called "The Wind,"
And the people shouted loud and long
For the master to play another song.
And the notes soared high.

Away from the crowd in a woodland glade,
All alone a greater master played
A sad, sad tune while the people slept.
But the willow bowed its head and wept
And so, too, did I.

*****Aola Seery, published at age 17,
Golden Harvest, Mistletoe Press, 1937*****

And Who Shall Say

The cup of sorrow stains His lips,
And pain cries in His eyes,
And blood cups in His outstretched palms,
And then our Savior dies ...

And who shall say His sorrow is
Not for us, and His pain ...
Not for the ones for whom He wept ...
Who doomed Him to be slain.

The cup of sorrow stains His lips,
And then our Savior dies,
But who shall say that pain killed love
Within our Savior's eyes?

The cup of sorrow stains His lips,
And deep He drinks of death,
But who shall say He did not cry
"Forgive," with His last breath?

My Multi-colored Mutt

Raggsy never saved a life or won a beauty prize.
He was just a multi-colored mutt
With lovelight in his eyes.
He looked as if he had been patched
With half a dozen furs,
Then rolled in mud and laid to dry
In a field of cockle-burrs.

Some bully of a bigger dog
Had taken half an ear.
The sight of Rags would make you laugh
And sometimes shed a tear
For half a dozen different furs,
And pathos, dirt, and soot
Made my funny, tragic little dog,
My multi-colored mutt.

But there were those who laughed the most
And said he should be shot,
And there were those who came and cried
And said that he should not.
Lots of dogs have beauty, but
Rag's gift was from above.
I could not find a single soul
Who'd care to shoot at love.

***** Aola Seery, published at age 17,
Golden Harvest, Mistletoe Press, 1937*****

Peasant's Prayer

A pool of azure set with stars,
A vast untroubled, friendly sea,
Succeeds the day with thought that bars
My simple mortal mind from Thee.
Let me live always, then as now,
In sheer and sweet simplicity.

All day I plowed the fertile plain.
The loam rose blackly from my plow,
And when I reap the yellowed grain,
I'll bow my head as I do now
In sheer and sweet simplicity.
Let me live always, then as now.

I'd like the humblest hut in heaven,
And when cold winter's rousted me,
I'd plant stars in azure furrows
And I'd serve Thee faithfully.
Let me live always, then as now,
In sheer and sweet simplicity.

*****Aola Seery, published at age 17,
Golden Harvest, Mistletoe Press, 1937*****

Hermit

I would have stillness at my side, for she and I are kin.
With stillness have I lived my life, and peaceful it has been,
With utter lack of loneliness, and they have wondered why,
Yet silent have I lived my life, and silent will I die.

Gray cavern walls are beautiful when lit by true faith's light,
And such a lamp can chase away the shadows of the night.
Great city streets and marbled halls and such I have not trod,
But I have lived with stillness and with peacefulness … and God.

I've never aided humankind, but I've learned how to pray,
And I have never harmed a man, nor gone the sinner's way.
I'll say to Him, "Dear God, I am a man of lowly worth,
But I've found rest in tumult and peacefulness on earth."

God's Handiwork

The mountain in the distance
Glistening with sun-kissed snow,
Sheds its tears into the forest
And the valley far below.

There it gushes forth in the fountains,
Like miniature seas,
Furnishing nectar for man and beast
And ambrosia for the trees.

Mountain and forest wrought by God,
And touched by his hands divine.
Man and animal side by side,
Brothers under the pine.

*****Written at age of 12 at Poteau, Oklahoma
Aola Seery, published at age 17,
Golden Harvest, Mistletoe Press, 1937*****

These Hands

I have no gifts to place at holy alters
Of myrrh, of frankincense, or even gold.
And in the midst of praying my voice falters.
My faith is not an anthem, full and bold,
Not like the rich and rolling organ tones,
Not like the still slow plowing of a river,
But like a small stream singing over stones,
The poignancy of harp strings set a-quiver.

I have naught but these hands as gifts for you,
These clumsy hands which break but yet can mend.
I give one to the Christ whose bleeding palms
Brought to a hate-filled world the name of friend.
I reach one hand to Christ ... the other one
To one who thinks he walks this world alone.
For when I do these things he must have done,
I feel my heart grow closer to God's son.

Philosophy

Always remember this, my dear, though the mills of the gods' grind slowly
That all comes to the patient ones and troubled waters clear.
The whole world only lives to die, and yet the dead are living.
He's happy who illusion has. Remember this, my dear.

And always keep your faith, my dear, for faith is mortal's anchor.
It keeps life's ship from off the rocks where dissolutions wraith
Sits breaking hearts and souls and minds in death and desolation.
Remember ever this, my dear, and always keep your faith.

*****Aola Seery, published at age 17,
Golden Harvest, Mistletoe Press, 1937*****

Guidance

God let my shallow soul to know
The peaceful hush and poetry
Of starless nights, winds blowing slow
That cross reaped fields in majesty
To cool the warm and fevered brow
Of one who followed long the plough,
Who kneels to hear the church bells,
Then takes him to thirst quenching spring
To find in silver brimming cup
The fount of youth whence godlings sup.

God let my selfish soul to see
The peace that guides the peasant's feet
And fills him with an ecstasy
O'er wind-made shadows in ripe wheat
And bids him toil 'neath rain and sun
With gladsome heart for work well done.
God strengthen more my heart and hand
That I may toil and till the land
To find on clear spring's mossy brink
I have the cream of life to drink.

**** *Aola Seery, published at age 17,*
Golden Harvest, Mistletoe Press, 1937****

The Things He Must Have Done

I'm glad that Jesus loved plain fisher folk,
And that I know he often chose to be
Among them when the heavy nets were drawn
Agleam with silver trophy from the sea.
He walked sweet, dew-wet paths at early dawn
Along the reedy margin of a shore.

He watched a frothy wave until it broke
Against the silent rhythm of an oar.
And then at dusk, around a campfire's glow
With Simon, Peter, Andrew, John, and James,
He blessed the bread and spoke some precious word
While glory dimmed the radiance of the flames.

I'm glad that it is given us to know
How Jesus found among his fellow men
These simple, quiet joys that must have stirred
His heart in much the way my own has been
Awake to beauty of the land and sea
And fellowship of loving company.

Golden Harvest

I had a tiny field where naught would grow
Save the weeping willow bending by the flow
Of a small brook leaping silver in the sun,
Laughing water that would clench the thirst of one.
And all the breezes of the night and day
Would sweep the tiny field and steal one's cares away.
"Henceforth," I said, "this field shall not be sown.
This tiny field I'll keep for God alone."

With spring my wealth increased a thousandfold
For my tiny field was turned to shining gold
With yellow flowers. Year to year they spread
'Til all my fields were one big flower bed.
A corner of my heart had naught within.
"Henceforth," I said, "it shall belong to Him."
And like the flowers and the field I set apart,
That small place grew until it filled my heart.

**** Aola Seery, published at age 17,
Golden Harvest, Mistletoe Press, 1937****

A Dream

I found a tiny fragment of a dream
Left from my childhood days, a dream so old
That the starshine had worn off and left it cold.
"Keep it," said a voice, "and watch it gleam."

I kept the dream although it wasn't bright
And found illusions lost so long ago,
Mended broken promises to make it glow,
And was rewarded with faith's shining light.

*****Aola Seery, published at age 17,
Golden Harvest, Mistletoe Press, 1937*****

The Cross Man

What have you done?
"I have been cross," he said and bowed his head,
   Silent at the whispering of wings.
The Examiner looked within his book and said,
   "Sometimes there are reasons for such things."

He had been cross, and twice the sound of warring
   Had sounded notes of anguish in his ears.
Born of two bloods and born for pain and crying,
   With poverty the harvest of his years.

He had been cross. Does not the earth in turning
   Hold tempests to its heart to which trees bow,
And with its weight of woe and flood and burning,
   Look out upon us with a furrowed brow?

But nothing said of gray-lit, not-yet mornings
   When soil slid blackly from his plow, for then
He was at peace with all the world, for plowing
   Brings God into the hearts of simple men.

And nothing said of loyalty and toiling
From dawn 'til dusk ... the tilling of the lands.
He took the talents God gave to his keeping
And made the most of them ... his two strong hands.

If he was cross, within the book is written
A record of a day when rage was hurled
By Christ, the Prince of Peace, within a temple
Against the moneychangers of the world.

The Examiner wrote within his book, and writing,
Said softly, "Heav'n is yours ... pass on my brother,"
And turned to ask his question of the next,
A Caesar of some century or other.
What have you done?

The Last Mile of the Way

I've traveled the path that leads to pain
And the path that leads to laughter.
I've known the pain of a loved one's death
And the strange deep silence after.
I gathered dreams from the wooded paths
At the dawn of my youthful day,
And now I know that their broken bits
Mark the very first mile of my way.

I followed a path through gilded clouds,
To find, as all dreamers do,
That the gilt rubs off and through its gold,
Black clouds come glooming through.
When I gathered dreams from the paths where I
At mid-morning was wont to stray,
I gave them all for a baby's smile ...
The second milestone on my way.

And mile by mile I have traveled the way,
And more often than not alone,
Seeking a seat at the Master's feet,
To kneel at His golden throne.
And my eyes have beheld a great vision,
And my mouth has found new words to say ...
With the strength of my soul, I press on to my goal
To win the next mile of the way.

And I know that my prayers will be answered
When the haze of the earth is pierced through,
For I know that I'll find there, in Heaven,
Some thing that a dreamer can do ...
And the broken dreams, heartaches, and sorrows
He'll take unto Him in that day,
And give me a world of tomorrows,
When I've gone that last mile of the way.

He Prays

Father in heaven, I have sinned against Thee
And am no longer worthy to be called Thine.
You gave me life and the world to take if I so willed.
You gave me your love and the love of my fellow man.
And then you gave unto my hand the miracle of time,
A chain of years, of precious years, and I have failed you.
Dear Father, I have wasted one of these years.
I have wasted it away. Part of it I have wasted
In disobedience of Thy word and part of it
In neglect of my fellow man. I have spoken no kind word,
Done no kind deed, and the year is gone, and I can see
What I have done. I come to Thee.

I know that I have yet another year.
Give me this chance to tear this page
From out the book of life and write again
In words of beauty on a whiter page,
If it be within my power to do so.
I have forgotten the way my errant feet should go,
The power to know sympathy and pity,
But perhaps if I should take this year and make it two
In deeds of kindness and in acts of worth …
I do not ask forgiveness, but the chance
To come again another year and say,
Here is what you gave unto my keeping,
I have used this wisely, Father, yes, and well.

God Understands

When a person's soul is too full for the saying,
Full to the point of physical pain,
When a person's thoughts are bound to go straying,
And one can't make one's meaning come out in the praying,
But just keeps repeating again and again
The same old words in the same old refrain,
God understands.

When faith and its glory are hidden from sight
By the darkness of doubt and the black of despair,
When it's time for the dawn, and the sun gives no light
Because faith is still struggling with shadows of night,
When one doesn't know the power of prayer
And looks for light but finds no light there,
God understands.

***** Aola Seery, published at age 17,
Golden Harvest, Mistletoe Press, 1937*****

You, Scientist

You, with your talk of polarization,
Roaring turbines, insulation,
Atom-smashers, amps DC,
Could learn so very much from me!

For I have learned hills turn on sky,
And rules to measure lifetimes by,
And sought to see the why of breath
And solve a simple problem ... Death.

Where dew drops tremble in the grass,
And cool winds breathe, and warm winds pass,
Would you not find in beating wings
An answer to the why of things?

Oh, Scientist, with eyes that see
Naught but wheels and theory,
Television, radio,
High Frequency ... if you should go

You have held lightning in your hand,
But I've remained close to the land.
You've robots and remote control.
I've answered this ... where goes my soul?

Re-Incarnation

I saw you bow, I saw you kneel,
To a chariot that was mine,
All clad in torn and filthy rags,
The tender of the swine.

I saw you with a shaven poll,
A scornful, selfish mien.
I touched you with a leper's hand
And begged you make me clean.

I saw you kneel, I heard you cry,
"A boon, my Lord, a boon."
I called out, "Varlets, run him down!
Run down the foul buffoon!"

You looked at me with cunning eyes ...
I recall it now this day ...
And asked in tones of pomp and greed,
"And what hast thou to pay?"

Today we're walking straight to God
   Where free men blazed the trail,
A poor man by a poor man's side …
   The light begins to fail,

For soon our spirits will stand straight
   And clean before His glance.
Our souls will kneel and, hand in hand,
   Thank Him for this last chance.

*****Aola Seery, published at age 17,*
Golden Harvest, Mistletoe Press, 1937****

The Ultimate

I knew that He would come because the spring
   Was green upon the hills and lush in hollows,
   And lilies lifted heads and called to swallows,
And the myriad other birds the spring winds bring.

I knew that He would come, and so I sought Him,
   And I searched o'er hill and meadow for my King.
I thought perhaps the whisp'ring winds had brought Him,
   But I failed to find him in the green-leafed spring.

I sought Him, and I searched and only found
   A sandaled footprint in the silver dew,
   A lily standing tall against the blue,
And small, sweet flowers starring mossy ground.

I sought Him, and I searched and thought I heard Him
   In the soft song of the wind and in the sound
   Of bare-limbed branches leafing, and I heard Him
In times between when the silence was profound.

Woven Threads

In His weaving of the world, He paused a space
And lest his fragile web be all for naught,
This mystic web of life so strangely wrought,
He wove a stronger thread into the lace,
A thread to strengthen dreams, ideals and thought.
A silken web with linen as its base,
Made strong with but a touch of commonplace
To add the trueness and the color that he sought.

In His weaving of the thread, He wove the souls
Of new-cut wood, well stacked and piled up high,
Of new-baked bread and cake and apple pie,
Of shasta daisies set in yellow bowls,
Of the burning sun in glaring summer sky,
Of the bell that on a Sunday morning tolls
And mixed with high ideals and dreams and goals.
And the whole was washed in love and hung to dry.

*****Aola Seery, published at age 17,
Golden Harvest, Mistletoe Press, 1937*****

Hoffman's Portrait of the Christ Child

There lies within Thine eyes of quietness,
Painted on a canvas, dimmed by time,
A beauty, and a depth of tenderness
That plays upon my soul-strings the sublime
And holy music of the Heavenly choir,
And brings unto mine eyes,
So strangely, tears,
And in my being, strange high thoughts arise,
Making of my soul a singing lyre,
And a nothing of a thousand and some years.

Thy hair, so loved by winds of Galilee,
Caught, and bound forever into place,
Has faded to a shadowed mystery,
A halo for the glory of Thy face,
And a thousand years are naught, and I can see
A little Child at play
In Nazareth,
Or teaching in the temple on that day,
Of things which were, and things someday to be
When a thousand and some years would seem a breath.

Thy mouth, dream-woven, melts half-smilingly
Into the shadows, and Thy lips, half-parted, seem
To hold compassion, and to know a sympathy
In my knowing, and my sharing of Thy dream.
They told me Jesus died upon the cross ...
He gave His life for men,
And dying, smiled.
How strange it was I did not know Him then.
How strange I did not know, not guess my loss,
Yet learned to love this thousand-year-old child.

Suburban Spring

Now it is May. Where once were sunlit fields
I see the paving shining in the sun.
The buttercup is lost to small square lawns.
The dandelion is dead. The grass has won.
The planter boxes bloom with purchased plants.
These blooms are not love-gathered treasured seeds,
But bought in all the urgency of spring,
The blossoming of our forgotten needs.
When I was six, I ran in sunlit fields
To flit from flower to flower in the sun,
A spirit freed from winter's chrysalis,
When it was May, and new life had begun,
And there was wonder in the sun-warm wind,
And solemn worship in the bending over
To pluck, without a fear, a golden bee
Drowsing on his honeyed throne of clover.

I scan the skies these days for alien wings.
I watch my children, fearful, from the door.
I fence them in with fear that progress brings,
And I am six times six, and then three more.
We live in quiet streets in quiet fear
And do not speak to strangers. Yet I know
A Stranger spoke to me and won my love
In sunlit fields, in May, and long ago,
And I have sought Him in the church and town,
And I have sought Him on my knees in prayer,
But never once, since I was six years old,
Have I been quite so sure that God was there.
So, I must bring my childhood to my child,
Warm sun-starred fields, and things newborn and small,
And show them God is here, and God is now.
We must look and listen harder, that is all.

———

Peter Was a Good Man

Peter was a good man. He came here, dazed by all
America's magnificence. That those trees, straight and tall,
That stood upon his land were his, he never understood.
He searched all down the countryside, and gathered bits of wood,
And bound them into faggots, while his great trees stood unscarred,
And he planted cabbages along the border of his yard.

Sometimes I think, on evenings when the wind makes moan,
I can see him tending cabbages where roses should have grown,
And I think I have seen him, when the mists lie low,
Seeking little sticks and twigs beneath the crusted snow.
Remembering his thriftiness, recalling how he gave,
I set a tiny apple tree above his unmarked grave.

I wonder if in Heaven, is his happiness complete?
If there are little sticks and twigs along the golden street …
If wings will substitute for feet that for the earth were made,
Or how a harp will sound in hands more suited to a spade.
Peter was a good man. I sometimes wonder though
If there is room in Heaven for cabbages to grow.

———

Summation

If we have written no name on this world
To live and sound in some far distant year,
If we have touched no single shining star,
Nor sung a song a great-grandchild might hear,
If we have left no footprints on this earth
To say, "Here once they walked, here once they stood,"
Yet we have shared and cared, grieved and believed,
And found that life is love, and love is good;
If we have built no temples out of stone,
If we have cast no bells to swing and chime,
We have planted trees to grow and shade and bear,
And sing God's praises for a little time.

If we have not seen all there is to see,
Nor spoken all the words that can be said,
Yet we have dreamed our dreams, have sought and thought,
Have given comfort and been comforted.
A word sometimes outlasts a temple wall.
We can leave the stars for younger eyes to see.
The young reach up for things 'til they grow tall
And know that they can reach eternity.
They join with us in writing on the world
The name of Friend and Brother, Father, Mother,
To build real love, like temples through the years,
And take turns giving faith, each to the other.

LOLA AOLA SEERY VANDERGRIFF

1920 - 1989

Aola Vandergriff was a life-long American poet and author, publishing her idealistic childhood poems at the age of 17. In the 1970s and 1980s she produced twenty New York Times bestselling gothic and historical romance novels under her own name and a pen name, Kitt Brown.

Aola was born Lola Aola Seery on a college campus in Le Mars, Iowa, to a teenage mother and one of the first electricians in the region. Her father's work took them from Kansas to Oklahoma when she was very small, where they struggled through the Great Depression. The family was aided by Aola's frequent cash prizes for her entries in the Denver Post's regular poetry contests. She launched her writing career at seventeen with the publication of a book of poems, *Golden Harvest*, which she also illustrated. Subsequently, she was dubbed "Oklahoma's Baby Poet" by Burton Rascoe, editor of Esquire magazine. As war loomed in Europe, Aola was reading her poetry on KTOK, Oklahoma City, to a large audience.

In the early 1940s, Aola became protégé to Jennie Harris Oliver, Oklahoma's Poet Laureate. Impressed with her artwork, Ms. Harris chose Aola to illustrate her book, *Pen Alchemy*. When America became embroiled in WW II, Aola married a young soldier, Bill Vandergriff, who later served in England and returned after the war to raise a family of six children with Aola.

As an adult, with her children nearly grown, Aola spoke at schools and various organizations and taught writing at American River College in Sacramento, California. She was also an associate editor for *Writer's Digest* and was interviewed many times in newspapers and on local and national television. She travelled extensively and carefully researched her historical novels and never ceased writing poetry. This collection was assembled by her children and consists of approximately 500 poems, including 100 poems from her 1937 book, *Golden Harvest*, her radio program, and a lifetime of turning to poetry to share her reflections on life, love, war and death.

Her novels are currently being republished by Sapere Books of Great Britain and released worldwide through Amazon, keeping her voice alive for a new generation.

Lola Aola Seery, 1941
(C. J. Kaho, Oklahoma Historical Society)

POEMS BY TITLE

A

A Chilling Rain	230
A Cradle Rocking	121
A Crooked Christmas Tree	157
A Dark Moon, Always	224
A Dream	397
A Farm Woman's Diary	136
A Flower from A Bride's Bouquet	55
A Garden	329
A Ghost	16
A Little House	147
A Man Wants a Son	242
A Moment There	239
A Mother's Vigil	280
A Name	80
A Rose	4
A Shield	66
A Stranger to These Ways	238
A Tree in a Trailer Window	158
A Valentine	76
A Wishing Kiss	60
A Woman Scorned	256
A Writer's Chains	176
Advice to a Young Poet	32
Again	280
All These Am I	10
Amulet	5
An Empire Falls	275
An Empty Heart	150
An Interview with Dame Nature	216
And Who Shall Say	389
Anew In Springtime	194
April	204
April Fool	218
Awkward Angel	185

B

Because Someone Did Not Forget	312
Belief	364
Bewitched	38
Bitter Autumn	233
Bittersweet	272
Black Earth Love	328
Blue Door to Nowhere	172
Blue Dream	60
Bondage	9
Borne on the Wind	120
Buried Treasure	254

C

Catalpa School, First Grade	109
Chained	30
Changeling	11
Cherokee Prophecy	311
Chilly Winds	233
Christmas, 1967	119
Claustrophobia	183
Cliff Dwelling	316
Close to the Stars	91
Coffee Break	87
Coffined	225
Color Line	307
Comparison	188
Compensation	54
Comrade Unremembered	297
Conformity	190
Cornerstone	48
Cornstalk Fiddle	337
Country Church	370
Creation	7
Crucifixion	374
Cycle	301
Czechoslovakia	292

POEMS BY TITLE

D

Day's End	338
Dear Dreamer	2
Dear Santa	156
Death Is Like a Paneled Door	358
Death of an India Rubber Man	174
Declining an Invitation to Dinner	146
Derelict	361
Desecration	310
Dictator	291
Discontent	236
Divorce - An Abstract Impression	246
Do Not Dream Back	268
Don't Be Afraid	356
Don't Let Your Heart Go South	274
Dream Clouds	33
Dream Riches	50
Dream Ship	4
Dream-Builder	49
Dream-Shiner-Upper	93
Dreams	31
Dress Rehearsal	15
Duel in Simmon's Swamp	295

E

Ebbtide	348
Effervescence	77
Elmiry	88
Enchanted Garden	324
Enchantment	6
Enough for Me	49
Eternal Change	198
Ever Since I Came	154
Every Day at Sundown	300

F

Fairy Grandmas	91
Fairy Music	218
Faith	160
Fall of the King	320
Fantasy	178
Farewell	127
Father-Mother	123
Fear	350
Featherstitched In Blue	92
Fences	149
Fiddle-Footed Cowpoke	90
Filing	239
First Love	59
First Snow	214
Five	84
Flying South	197
Folded Wings	360
Following a Star	92
Fools	354
Footsteps	237
For Jesus	367
Forgotten Youth	235
Foundations	388
Four Ages	139
Freeway	200
Futility	144

G

Genius	177
Ghost Child's Face	269
Ghost House	152
Ghost-Love	227
Glory	376

POEMS BY TITLE

God Understands 403
God's Child 284
God's Handiwork 392
God's World 386
Golden Harvest 396
Grapevine Swing 81
Grow Old Gracefully 336
Growing Blind 247
Growing Weather 339
Guidance 394

H

Half-A-Child 257
He Prays 402
Heartbreak at Six 84
Hearth Fire 56
Her 'n' Me 142
Her Hands 140
Here Are My Dreams 63
Heritage 193
Heritage of Hills – Class of 1939 128
Hermit 391
High Noon 368
Him Will I Love 62
Hoffman's Portrait of the Christ Child . 407
Hold Hard to All Good Things 276
Holland, May 14th, 1940 293
Home 151
Home at Twilight 364
Home Work 207
Homecoming 56
Hospital Waiting Room 357
Housework 182
How Does Your Garden Grow? 325
How Much I Envy You 94

I

I 188
I Am Gypsy 36
I Am I 13
I Am the Very Only Fairy 202
I Fain Would Dance 28
I Found Peace 379
I Must Remember 253
I Remember a Time 193
I Sat Upon a Quiet Hill 279
I Saw the Child King 162
I Shall Not Miss You 254
I Shall Write Again 249
I Thee Endow 71
I Wish I Knew 226
I Wonder 16
I Would Like to Write 14
I, Who Remember 265
If I Could Build a Mind 15
If I Should Go 346
If This Be Your Idea 181
If You Should Go to Fight 274
In the Hollows 206
In This Room 102
Indecision 3
Independence Day 290
Indian Maid 309
Information 67
Insight 347
Intentions 179
Interior Decorating 149
It Will Not Seem Strange 265

POEMS BY TITLE

J
Jeweled Hill 204
Joe Bill Garrett 184
John Smith – 1880 to 1929 303
Judgment Day 380
Just That Way 70

K
Katie of the Salt Marsh 258

L
La Selva Encantada 203
Ladder of Life 138
Ladies 10
Last Night 192
Last Night I Dreamed 242
Laughter 194
Leaves 198
Lend Lease 277
Leopold 276
Lessons in Kite Flying 83
Limitations 327
Little Boy Lost 372
Little Papoose 314
Little, Dirty, Ragged Urchin 115
Living 8
Lost Mother 93
Love Triangle 97
Lullaby 124
Lullaby Lady 108

M
Ma! 94
Madonna in a Blue Gown 110
Man of Galilee 369
Man-Made 377
March 205
Memories 195

Mermaid and Mortal 28
Might Have Been 245
Milady 94
Mirror of Life 204
Mirror, Mirror 73
Mist Against the Window 264
Mist o' Magic 12
Monuments 300
Moods 8
Moon Madness 107
Moon Tears 208
Mother 86
Mother - Poet 185
Mother-Fond 96
Mother's China Plate 126
Mother's Prayer 181
Mourning 234
Mud Pies 82
Mushroom Towns 212
My Friend, Storm 322
My Gifts 18
My Goblin Child 85
My Heart Lies in the Sun 175
My House 151
My Life Had Need 74
My Masterpiece 40
My Multi-colored Mutt 390
My Prayer 382
My Sins and I 187
My Sun, My Moon, My Stars 47

N
Never Cry 240
New Fields 200
New Lamps for Old 62
New Years – 1937 166

POEMS BY TITLE

Nine Pins 352	Prayer Perfect 366
No Less a King 104	Prelude 72
Northland 203	Prisoner 355
Not for This 378	Problem in Higher Mathematics 182
Not the Way of You 352	Prodigy 89
Now 248	Progress 212
Now in November 348	Promises 64

O / Q

October's Oklahoma 330	Quadropotamus 178
Of Kingdoms 120	Queen for a Day 26
Of Kings and Courage 266	Queer Heart 19
Oklahoma Father 134	Quest 248
Old Trails 222	Quilts 114
On Her Wedding Day 51	
One Brief Hour of April 211	**R**
One Candle 159	Rain 302
One Dream 334	Re-Incarnation 404
One God 308	Refugees 98

P

	Remembering Wee Homes 148
Pagan 5	Reserve 68
Pals 184	Resurrection 365
Pastel Fairies 349	Retirement 140
Peace 378	Retribution 250
Peaceful Hollow 216	Revenge 189
Peacemaker 288	Reverie in Rain 338
Peasant's Prayer 391	Roses and Thorns 26
Perfection 241	Royalty 197
Peter Was a Good Man 410	**S**
Philosophy 393	Sacrilege 153
Pioneers 373	Salute 214
Pockets 88	Salvation 384
Portrait from a Castle Wall 228	School Days 117
Prairie Pictures of Autumn 199	Schoolyard 97
Prairies 217	Scottish Ballad 245
Pray, Be Kinder 251	Second Helping 52
Prayer 376	Secrets 188
	Seeking an Ember 232

POEMS BY TITLE

Selling Memories	260	The Beckoning Light	146
Shadow - Bond	270	The Black Pony	321
Shadows	132	The Bride	64
Shells	29	The Cabbage and the Rose	186
Short Short Story	180	The Color of His Eyes	46
Silences	57	The Comforter	24
Sing Me a Love Song	139	The Confederate	299
Singing Bird	317	The Credulous	32
Singing in the Sun	362	The Cross Man	398
Snow	322	The Disillusioned	266
Somebody's Spoiled the Baby	116	The Door to My Heart	224
Somehow I Do Remember	264	The Dream	31
Someone Should Have Told You	261	The Drum	112
Sometimes	258	The Eagle and the Dove	315
Soul-Strings	359	The Empty Stocking	164
Sounds	20	The Entrance to Fairy Land	215
Spinster	241	The Fiddler	111
Spiritual Rest	361	The Fisher's Wife	244
Spring	194	The Fisherman	366
Spring Comes Out of January	340	The Gallery	326
Star Wishes	147	The Gift of Flowers	372
Stay at Home	25	The Grandeur of Spain	298
Still Those Tints Abide	336	The Great Master	389
Storm	9	The House That Jack Built	168
Stormy	85	The Last Mile of the Way	400
Suburban Spring	408	The Last Whip-Poor-Will	271
Summation	411	The Letter	58
Summer's Child	22	The Little Hills	341
Sunbonnet Sue	342	The Message	374
Sunset	206	The Name of Spain	288
Survival	189	The New Year	165
T		The Old Ways	105
Temptation	175	The Poet	52
Thank You Note	219	The Precipice of Silence	252
Thanksgiving	154	The Quiet Hour	331

POEMS BY TITLE

The Return	387	*Thoughts*	24
The Right to Bear Arms	278	*Three in a Room*	34
The Second Prayer	262	*Through the Centuries*	42
The Shadow Place	289	*Through the Gap in the Hedge*	170
The Shadowed Stair	346	*Tiger, Tiger*	95
The Shepherd	150	*Tintype*	54
The Sneep	174	*Tiptoe Time*	91
The Song of the Pinewood Tree	351	*To a Teenage Son*	113
The Star	155	*To a Tom Tom*	313
The Stranger	46	*To an Erring Relative*	185
The Things He Must Have Done	395	*To Fifty Years*	358
The Tiniest Evergreen	160	*To Hear You*	181
The Touch of His Hand	375	*To Know You Are There*	53
The Trillipede	177	*To Michael*	99
The Ultimate	405	*To Question Why*	348
The Unicarp	179	*To Whom It May Concern*	306
The Wanderer Returns	213	*Today*	242
There Is No Place	234	*Together*	61
There is Such a Thing	69	*Tonight*	226
These Hands	392	*Trail of Tears*	316
They	17	*Trampled Dreams*	294
They Say	180	*Transformation*	255
Thirst	282	*Trisexoderm*	179
This Gift for Life's December	63	*Turn About*	176
This Is My Sign	343	*TV*	180
This Is the Day	118	*Two Loves*	68
This is the Sea	320	*Two Mothers*	285

POEMS BY TITLE

Two Songs 220
Two-Ways-Going 240

U

Unclaimed Treasure 176
Understanding 335
Unstrung 250

V

Valentines Day – 1918 296

W

Waiting 262
Wanted: A House 169
War 281
Waterlogged 183
Wee Know-Nothing-Curly-Head 106
What Broke Then? 271
What Shadows Do 183
What to Name the Baby 125
When Day Brings 48
When They Are Near 70
When Today is Yesterday 210
When You Are Away 58
Where I Shall Lie 349
Where Shamrocks Grow 353
While Others Sleep 133
Whip-Poor-Will 323
Whisperings Among the Leaves 2
White Mist Rising 308

Who Goes There? 286
Who Tends a Tree 122
Why 100
Why Do I Sigh? 230
Why Do I Weep? 231
Why Have You Come to Awaken Me? ... 247
Will-o'-the-Wisp 23
Wings 192
Wings for Her Feet 141
Wings of the Wind 40
Winter 229
Winter Respite 135
Wisdom 89
With Only Wonder 267
Woman's World 143
Words Unspoken 59
Would-be Sinner 180
Woven Threads 406

Y

Yesterday 229
You Grieve - I Sing 360
You Will Not Know 263
You, I Love 201
You, Oklahoma 196
You, Scientist 404
You, Who Lived Here 148

www.ingramcontent.com/pod-product-compliance
Lightning Source LLC
Chambersburg PA
CBHW032145080426
42735CB00008B/594